Ancient Forest International

Chile's Native Forests
A Conservation Legacy

Ken Wilcox

This publication was funded in part by a grant from
The Weeden Foundation

Special thanks also to
Betty M. Anderson

Chile's Native Forests
A Conservation Legacy
Ken Wilcox

Published in the USA for AFI by
NW Wild Books *in association*
with North Atlantic Books *All
rights reserved. Brief excerpts
may be reprinted without
permission if credit is given.*

ISBNs 1-55643-234-8
       0-9617879-2-9

Printed on 100% recycled paper

Photographers:
   Kiko Anderson
   Alex Clapp
   Dan Dancer
   Douglas Fir
   Steve Gilroy
   Adriana Hoffmann
   Greg King
   Rick Klein
   Craig Marks
   Peter McBride
   Dennis Murphy
   Eric Nill
   Galen Rowell
   Kim Sallaway
   Harold Schlange
   Ken Wilcox
Cover photos:
   Greg King *(front)*
   Dan Dancer *(back)*
Maps & artwork by:
   Lisa K. Beck
Tree silhouettes courtesy of:
   Adriana Hoffmann & the
   Claudio Gay Foundation
Layout/design:
   Ken Wilcox & Kathy Glass

Direct inquiries to:
   ANCIENT FOREST
   INTERNATIONAL (AFI)
   P. O. Box 1850
   Redway, CA 95560 USA

Araucaria,
Chile's National Tree
❀ Dan Dancer

Warmest regards to all who helped bring this
project to fruition. The work is dedicated to all my friends
in Chile, and to the Chonos people, a nomadic
canoe culture of the northern fiords of Chilean Patagonia
who greeted with compassion the plunderers of
the New World. Their culture of dalcas, sealskins, fire,
mussels, mushrooms, huts, harpoons, and the telling
of tales around remote hotsprings is lost forever.
Yet the rich world that sustained them for thousands
of years is still with us. May it never slip away.

Ken Wilcox
January, 1996

Contents

FRONT COVER: *Cañi Forest Sanctuary, Lakes District, Chile.*   ❀ Greg King
BACK COVER: *Valdivian Rainforest, southern Andes, Chile.*   ❀ Dan Dancer
← *Princess Falls, above the Bío-Bío River, central Chile.*   ❀ Ken Wilcox

Morning in the southern Andes.   ❀ Steve Gilroy

Preface

This report on Chilean native forest conservation has been compiled for use by North American and international environmental organizations and others who are concerned with native forest issues in Chile or in Latin America generally. We hope this overview will benefit both new and ongoing native forest conservation efforts.

We also hope that it gives the reader a better understanding of the global importance of the old forests of the southern hemisphere; that it helps bring useful information across language and other cultural barriers; and that it effectively reduces the great distance between Chilean forests and conservation resources in North America.

The information is based on extensive research and interviews conducted in Chile and the U.S. between 1989 and 1994. Much credit is due, not only to government officials, forest ecologists and environmental activists in Chile, but to the people who live and work in these regions and who were eager to share their sentiments regarding the vulnerable state of the nation's remaining virgin forests.

Contacts in Chile included people in science, academics, government, the forest industry, the environmental community and native people. Every effort has been made to convey their concerns, experience and suggestions throughout the text of this report.

Several outstanding organizations in Chile, the Comite Nacional pro Defensa de la Fauna y Flora (CODEFF), Fundación Lahuen, Defensores del Bosque Chileno, Bosque Antiguo, and the Foundation for Education, Science, and Ecology (EDUCEC) are all dedicated to the preservation of Chile's native forests. The energy and expertise they provide have been instrumental to the cause and we invite everyone to support their efforts.

Ancient Forest International sponsored this project through the financial support of The Weeden Foundation and Betty M. Anderson. We are especially grateful to Alan Weeden and James Sheldon for their commitment to the cause of Chilean forests and for seeing this work to completion. Gratitude is also expressed to Wildwings, Ladeco Airlines and to Steve Anderson's Chile Information Project (CHIP).

Many individuals offered invaluable assistance to this project. Special kudos (in no particular order) to Rick Klein, Hernán Verscheure, Erika Guerrero, Adriana Hoffmann, Pablo Donoso, Claudio Donoso, Kathy Glass, Ami Goldberg, Douglas Fir, Lisa Beck, John Moriarty, Claudia González, Daniel González, Sara Rodgers, Carlos Weber, Ziley Mora, Juan Armesto, Cecilia Smith, Kim Sallaway, Peter Childs, Esteban Millard, Mishka Straka, Fred Bauer, John Jennings, Peter McBride, Kiko Anderson, Nayaret Quezada, Gustavo Gutierrez, Antonio Lara, Byron Swift, Mauricio Fierro, Rod Del Pozo, and Graham Lewis.

Alerce
Fitzroya cupressoides

Giant alerce, southern Andes.   ❋ Galen Rowell

Foreword

AT THE END OF THE TWENTIETH CENTURY there are few places left in the world that are still pure. The *wild* is scarce. The African poet Baba Dioum said that "In the end we will conserve that which we love. We will love that which we understand. And we will understand that which we are taught." This book shares some of what Chileans and others have learned about one of Earth's wildest places. It was written to increase awareness and appreciation for Chile's pristine and exuberant native forests.

Our greatest common threat today is not nuclear proliferation but rather ecosystem degradation—and its corollary tragedy, species extirpation. As the human population grows, nature is continually degraded and the urgency builds to save what is left, be it seed stock, whales or primary forest. These things are irreplaceable. They are not making any more wilderness.

It is not surprising that the old-growth logging industry would have us believe (as would the whaling nations) that sustained harvest is possible on a large scale. But people who do not make their living from giant whales or ancient trees often disagree. It has been calculated that if a dollar was borrowed to plant a tree and the dollar was paid back at the going rate during a 400-year production cycle, the tree would eventually be worth $1.3 trillion. Old-growth ecosystems are priceless. They are not, in human terms, renewable.

We have taken all of the primary forest we dare. In light of Earth's present grumblings and rumblings, warnings and warmings we find two options: to act locally and to act globally. While bioregionalism is the ideal, transnationalism is the deal. Conservationists must know how to cross borders. In a world where a junk bondsman can destroy a distant forest he has never seen, conservationists have a responsibility to act on behalf of forests everywhere.

We now understand that the sea and the sky are global commons which help sustain the biosphere's quality of life. We are close to understanding this about Earth's forests as well. Viewing the great sylvan tracts of Amazonia, Borneo, Siberia, British Columbia and Chile as integral parts of the global commons is not a threat to private property or national sovereignty. In fact, this enlightened perspective contributes to the security of both. Environmental degradation is the real threat.

Unlike other South American countries, virtually all of Chile's forests are temperate, not tropical. Earth's few remaining temperate rainforests are truly ancient forests — in terms of the average age of its trees — and Chile's trees and groves are the oldest of them all. Today, the opportunity to walk for days among living things as old as the Sphinx is possible only in Chile.

Chile's *Bosque Valdiviano* may be Earth's most extensive pristine temperate rainforest, within which are recesses never known to be visited by humans. The age of the trees and biomass of the rainforest make the Chilean "cold jungle" one of the most successful biomes ever studied. A report published by Ecotrust in 1992 found Chile's temperate rainforest to be the most species-diverse. Over two-thirds of the native plants are endemic and many are considered rare or endangered.

For those of us at Ancient Forest International who are involved in the Southern Cone environmental arena it is still difficult to believe that, as recently as 1988 when AFI began its expeditions deep into the unexplored rainforest regions of southern Chile, the international scientific and conservation communities were relatively unaware of this distant treasure. No non-governmental organization anywhere was exclusively dedicated to safeguarding it.

The timing is urgent. Chilean sources estimate that native forests are being destroyed or damaged by people and livestock at the rate of 120,000 to 200,000 hectares per year. Foreign investments in the Chilean forest industry are increasing at a vigorous pace. The nation's Congress, in response to national sentiment for protecting forests and determined to chart Chile's course free from foreign control, is now debating a new national forest law (a document U.S. and Canadian forestry agencies are advised to read).

CONAF, Chile's national park and forest service, helped create a system of protected wildlands that is the envy of richer nations. Yet the agency is underfunded and overextended. Of the 83 floristic formations identified in Chile, one-third remain unprotected in the wildlands system. The rich forests of Regions IX and X, where most of Chile's forest biomass and biodiversity occur, are among the least protected. The *Siempreverde*, the most biologically complex of the twelve principal forest types in Chile, contains the greatest diversity of species but is poorly protected. Similar Mediterranean temperate rainforests occur in only three other places on the planet. Each should be a high priority on any international conservation agenda.

Although much work remains, a lot has already been accomplished. AFI extends its highest appreciation to CONAF and the important work of Carlos Weber and others in the ongoing development of the National System of Protected Wildlands.

Within the environmental community, none have achieved more than CODEFF (*Comite Nacional pro Defensa de la Fauna y Flora*) in advancing the cause of native forest conservation in Chile. Under the leadership of Hernán Verscheure, CODEFF, the nation's largest and oldest environmental organization, helped galvanize an environmentally concerned citizenry into an active force for protecting Chile's ecological treasures into the next century. Weber and Verscheure are major players in shaping the future of forest policy in the country. Two more dedicated champions of environmental responsibility cannot be found.

The Lahuen Foundation, established in 1991, is rapidly becoming one of the most important native forest conservation organizations in Chile. Its original mission was to acquire and preserve primary forest for posterity. The focus today is environmental education and identifying sustainable alternatives to forest exploitation.

In 1993, forest activists in Chile organized *Defensores del Bosque Chileno* (Defenders of the Chilean Forest), also dedicated to the preservation of native forests. In the short time since its inception, Defensores has helped considerably to increase public awareness of the ongoing threats to native forests. Behind the empassioned leadership of botanist Adriana Hoffmann, perhaps Chile's best known scientist, *Defensores* is the group to watch. This alliance of leading intellectuals (Isabel Allende, Humberto Maturano, Manfreed Maxneef) comprises the country's most visible activist NGO.

As with many worthy pursuits, there is a gulf between what we want and what we can reasonably expect to achieve. This is no reason to lower our sights, however. Our historic relationship with the Earth has been that of *conqueror*. Our challenge is to become *caretaker*. Whether we call our home World, Earth, Gaia or Mother, we are in need of a new vision for the global environment. A new question being asked is not what we are going to do about the planet, but what is it going to do about us?

John Muir observed that nature is the only experience that consistently holds our interest, from infancy to old age. Great forests are fascinating places, much more than biological and genetic repositories or vast carbon sinks. They are spiritual sanctuaries that revitalize us. These we must keep. Because of their tremendous commercial value the most accessible ancient forests in the world are gone. Where can one go and still experience this kind of primordial wildness? Fortunately, there are still places, in Chile.

It is our highest hope that this document will serve to increase your understanding, appreciation and even love for one of Earth's most venerable living systems, and inspire you to act on behalf of endangered wilderness everywhere.

Rick Klein, AFI
Redway, California
1995

Forest
Regions
of
Chile

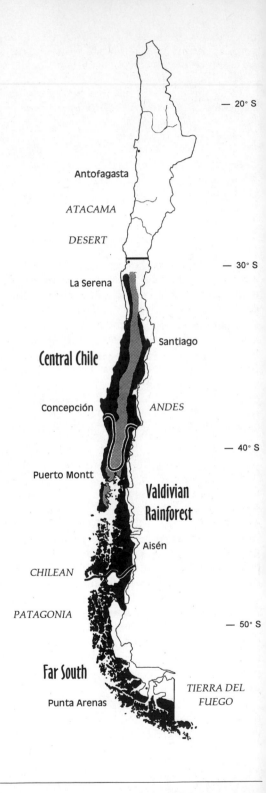

— 20° S

Antofagasta

ATACAMA

DESERT

— 30° S

La Serena

Santiago

Central Chile

Concepción

ANDES

— 40° S

Puerto Montt

Valdivian Rainforest

Aisén

CHILEAN

PATAGONIA

— 50° S

Far South

Punta Arenas

TIERRA DEL FUEGO

 Mostly Forested

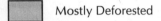 Mostly Deforested

☐ Mostly Non-Forested
(Desert, steppe, alpine)

Part 1

Native Forests of Chile

THAT REMARKABLE PART OF EARTH we know as Chile consists of an extraordinary diversity of environments, from the hottest and driest deserts to the coolest and wettest rainforests. The country spans nearly 40 degrees of latitude and more than 7,000 meters (22,800 feet) of vertical relief. Chile is 4,300 kilometers (2,600 miles) long and barely 160 kilometers (100 miles) wide, yet its Pacific coastline stretches farther than 10,000 km (6,200 miles) from Peru to the southern tip of South America. Two thousand volcanoes and cinder cones grace the eastern skyline where the crest of the Andes forms the international boundary with Argentina. If you could overlay a map of Chile across western North America, it would cover everything west of the coastal mountain ranges from Acapulco, Mexico, to Ketchikan, Alaska.

Within this unique landscape, nature has produced some of the world's most impressive forests. Among them, scarce groves of Chilean palms in the north; the widely distributed (and heavily exploited) southern beech or *Nothofagus* forests; the distinctive araucaria forests of south-central Chile, home to Chile's national tree; and the alerce/southern beech rainforests of the south. The giant alerce or "redwood of the Andes" is now recognized as one of the largest trees in the world and is the second-most long-lived tree known to botanists (California's bristlecone pine is the oldest).

These vast forests were, for the most part, still intact when the Spanish conquistadors first laid eyes on them in the sixteenth century. Undoubtedly, some had already been burned or cleared by indigenous people living in the lowlands. The natives opened the forest for agriculture, for grazing animals and for settlements, then celebrated with the great spirits who provided them with this wealth of resources.

As the Spaniards established their stronghold in central Chile, they cleared the land much more aggressively — and for similar reasons — but with much less humility. For them, the trees offered

Queule

(Gomortega keule), a stout broadleaf evergreen from central Chile, was once valued for its attractive wood grain and a fruit that native people used to make marmalade. Its range has largely been converted to pine plantations. An endemic species, queule has become so scarce that it is listed as an endangered species and is protected by law in Chile as a Natural Monument. It is also one of CONAF's highest priorities for preservation.*

* *Corporación Nacional Forestal, or CONAF, is an agency of the Agriculture Ministry which oversees the national park and protected areas system and regulates forestry activity in Chile.*

a convenient source of charcoal that could be used for heating and cooking, and for smelting copper, silver and gold. Native wood was used for mining timbers, building construction, furniture-making and, of course, fuelwood. The Spanish also burned forests deliberately in order to eliminate safe refuge for the natives. Yet, the total area of forest impacted in those years was insignificant compared to the relentless surge of destruction that would begin almost three centuries later.

Not long after Chile gained its independence from Spain in 1818, immigrants from Europe arrived *en masse* to settle the fertile promised land of southern Chile. The native forests, great "inexhaustible" stands of hardwoods and softwoods, were cleared to obtain building materials and to make room for crops, livestock, towns, railroads and carriageways. Tens of thousands of hectares of forest vanished around new and expanding population centers. Beginning in the late 1800s, vast stands of roble *(Nothofagus obliqua)* were felled to obtain raw material for the bridges, trestles and ties required by advancing railroads. During the same period, near Puerto Montt, a huge rainforest of ancient alerce containing the largest and oldest trees in South America, if not the entire world, was burned by German immigrants simply to get it out of the way.[1] The land proved much too swampy for cultivation or pasture and lies fallow still — a virtual wasteland.

The adverse impacts of settlement were not limited to forests. Land-clearing at this scale disrupted, displaced and, in the worst case, destroyed native cultures in much the same way that native Americans were stripped of their lands and freedom on the northern continent. By the turn of the century, indigenous populations in Chile had been reduced by at least ninety percent, a trend echoed throughout the New World.[2] By 1900, virgin forests had been cleared or substantially degraded for a distance, north to south, of nearly 1,500 kilometers.

In the 1940s, huge river valleys and nearby mountain slopes in the far south were set afire to open up new areas to livestock grazing. (At least 300,000 hectares has burned nationwide since 1986.) The first fields of non-native Monterey pine also began to appear in the mid-1900s. Thirty years later, massive pine plantations had spread throughout central Chile. By 1990, well over a million hectares of land once covered with native forest were committed to plantations.[3] World demand for Chilean wood chips and pulp has virtually exploded since 1987, with Japanese multinational corporations leading the way in forest exploitation.

While plantations are currently providing most of the softwood fiber, the chip industry poses an enormous threat to native forests, including both softwoods and hardwoods.

Deforestation in Chile is, in some ways, a familiar story, one that has been repeated many times over in nearly all forested

Southern beech (Notho-
fagus) *forest, somewhat
degraded by logging.*
❀ Ken Wilcox

regions of the world. Perhaps what is unique about Chile is the swift pace of destruction and the exceptional quality and diversity of trees that were and still are being destroyed.

The total area of deforestation in Chile is probably on the order of 15-20 million hectares, although no one knows precisely how much land is now or once was forested.* Estimates suggest that Chile's forests now cover about 15 million hectares,[4] an area half the size of Ecuador. However, as much as half this amount has already been cut over, degraded by fire or livestock, or replaced with pine or eucalyptus plantations. Perhaps only one-fourth of the forests still standing can be considered relatively undisturbed.

Most of the remaining virgin forests are the least accessible stands: those on the higher slopes of the Andes in central Chile, in isolated valleys and slopes of the southern coastal ranges, and in the largely uninhabited southern fiord region. A sizeable portion of the latter has been protected in the form of national parks and reserves, while the international forest industry is setting its sights on the rest—last remnants of the great diversity and biomass that once graced the lowlands.

It is not an exaggeration to say that Chile's remaining forest ecosystems are among the most poorly protected temperate forests on Earth. Their future appears dismal by some accounts, hopeful by others. In a world that seems intent on degrading or eliminating natural forests as quickly as possible, the last of Chile's native forests are, at last, being recognized internationally by foresters, biologists and ecologists as endangered ecosystems of global significance.[5]

* *Comprehensive evaluations of native forest distribution and composition are ongoing in Chile though far from complete. It may be several years before reliable statistics and accurate maps of all forest types become available. Therefore, the approximations provided here should not be misinterpreted as conclusive.*

Belloto del Sur

(Beilschmiedia berteroana),
an endangered species, is
another large endemic tree
whose range has been
severely reduced by agri-
culture. As little as a few
hundred acres are all that
remain, a condition that
has compelled CONAF to
give it the highest priority
for protection of any tree in
Chile. Belloto del sur is
legally protected as a
Natural Monument.

Native Forest Ecosystems

The ecological importance of Chile's forests rests in part on the fact that Chile is, biologically, an "island" isolated from the rest of South America by the Andean cordillera, the Atacama Desert (driest in the world) and the Pacific Ocean. Natural migration of plants and animals into or out of Chile is not easy. For millions of years, changes in climate and landscape have influenced the development of highly endemic communities of organisms. In fact, more than half of all native plants in Chile are found nowhere else in the world.[6]

Much of Chile's unique species diversity is apparent in the forests that emerged with the retreat of continental glaciers some 10,000 years ago. The central forests began to develop in a mild, Mediterranean climate much like that of central California. In the northernmost valleys, they tend to be dry, *sclerophyllous* forests with open canopies. An increasingly wet climate to the south supported the development of an unusual variety of broadleaf evergreen and deciduous trees, dominated by southern beech *(Nothofagus spp.)*, an ancient inhabitant of Gondwanaland, the southern supercontinent.

Farther south an even wetter and cooler climate produced a rare *temperate rainforest*, one of only a handful that exist on the

Chile's Shrinking Forest...

The original extent of natural forest in Chile is uncertain. Like most forested regions of the world, clearing for agriculture and settlement began hundreds and even thousands of years ago—long before there were any maps, photographs or written records of the immense forests that once graced the landscape.

To reconstruct the story of forest destruction, experts look for clues in existing forest cover and soils, they study climate conditions, species adaptations, evidence of fire, and draw upon local knowledge and historical accounts—a formidable challenge for any student of the forest.

Claudio Donoso, eminent forest ecologist at University Austral in Valdivia, has produced the best historic account yet available, entitled

Modificaciones del Paisaje Chileno a lo Largo de la Historia (1983). Says Donoso:

Forest ecosystems are subject to modifications derived from natural factors... [and from] the action of man... the destruction of the environment and the rupture of [natural] equilibrium... Obviously, in the early times, small populations and rudimentary technologies known and utilized would not permit human groups to exercise significant action over the forests. That contrasts with the action, generally destructive, capable of being produced [today] over natural environments by excessive masses of human population.... The great extensions of forests that covered the land promoted the idea in

planet. Large temperate rainforests comparable to Chile's are only found in the Pacific Northwest region of North America, New Zealand's South Island and Australia's island state of Tasmania.

The Chilean rainforest is largely comprised of southern beech, plus the last remaining stands of ancient alerce *(Fitzroya cupressoides)*. A striking difference between the cool temperate rainforests of Chile and Oceania and those of the northern hemisphere is the preponderance of broadleaf evergreens in the southern latitudes instead of conifers. The giant old trees, however, draped in epiphytes and engulfed in a thick green understory, are equally impressive in both hemispheres.

Chile's forests to this day are still developing and evolving into functioning communities of plants and animals engaged in an almost imperceptible dance with eternity. As time passes and conditions change, new and improved life forms emerge while others fade or slowly migrate to more suitable environments. Yet, the subtle forces of nature that are continually transforming the environment seem almost insignificant compared to the profound effects that industrialized civilization can bring to a forest — soil erosion, species extirpations, deforestation.

To understand the long-term implications that large-scale exploitation has for Chile's shrinking forests, we are obliged to learn all we can about the composition, physical structure and natural dynamics at work in the wild forests that still stand today. Ongoing research, model projects, and monitoring will help us learn how to exploit forest resources sensibly, while preserving the integrity and future viability of all forest ecosystems.

Ruil

(Nothofagus allessandri), also in the central region, is an extremely rare tree, also designated a Natural Monument, with no known survivors of mature age. Endemic to Chile, its highly fragmented populations have been listed as <u>endangered</u>. Ruil produces a strong, rot-resistant fiber that was once a lumber of choice for boat-building. It is fast-growing and ideally suited to forest recovery projects. With successful reforestation and ecosystem-based management, the tree offers outstanding commercial potential.

people... that forests were inexhaustible... today they are in a critical condition...

Original forests, estimated at close to 30 million hectares, were reduced by more than 20 percent between 1540 and 1900, an era encompassing colonization by Spain and later settlement by other Europeans.

The native forest shrank by another third or more this century to its present area of some 15 million hectares. Current losses are estimated to be in the range of 120,000 to 200,000 hectares each year, much of it involving conversions to non-native pine and eucalyptus plantations. If recent trends continue, additional losses could begin to upset the natural equilibrium of some forest ecosystems beyond the point of recovery.

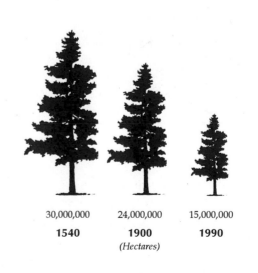

30,000,000	24,000,000	15,000,000
1540	**1900**	**1990**
	(Hectares)	

This recently burned-over forest in south-central Chile will likely be replanted with non-native pine.
❀ Steve Gilroy

"The interrelationship of environmental constituents determines the original development of the ecosystem... maintaining balance between the elements depends on the dynamic and natural equilibrium existent in nature. This balance is delicate, and in many cases still not fully understood."

—Adriana Hoffmann,
FLORA SILVESTRE
DE CHILE [1982]

Chilean foresters tend to describe today's native forests in terms of a dozen *forest types*, all of which are administered by the government forestry agency, *Corporación Nacional Forestal* or *CONAF*.[7] Each forest type and its predominant tree species are listed on page 12. All native forests are managed on the basis of rules and regulations adopted for each classification.

Ecologists, on the other hand, have described at least 33 kinds of forest ecosystems based on a total inventory of 83 distinct *floristic formations* identified in Chile.[8] These are also listed in the following pages. Both these and CONAF's forest types are discussed only briefly in this work. (Consult references at the end of the book for more detailed descriptions of specific forest ecosystems.)

CONAF

CONAF is a government agency comparable to the U.S. Forest Service and National Park Service combined. It is responsible for the management of protected areas and other public lands and oversees timber harvest activities on public and, more importantly, private land where the vast majority of commercial forestry in Chile occurs.

Coastal siempreverde rainforest; ulmo trees in bloom.
❀ Ken Wilcox

Native Forest Regions & Forest Types

For discussion purposes, Chile's native forests have been divided into three broad regions: *Central Chile*, the *Valdivian Rainforest* and the *Far South*. The technical shortcomings of this or any other organizational scheme that might be used must be acknowledged. However, this approach was selected for the benefit of non-technical readers. General forest types and floristic formations found within each region are listed on the next two pages.

Chile's forests are highly varied and complex communities of life which, like most ecosystems, do not possess clear boundaries. Thus, the maps contained in this overview are only general representations of the natural range of the twelve forest types. Each is touched on briefly in the following sections.

Roble

(*Nothofagus obliqua*), although heavily exploited, is another large, fast-growing tree that does well in a variety of environments. A deciduous species, it can survive at very high altitudes (more often the domain of lenga and araucaria) as a stunted or deformed tree. Its valuable wood is rot-resistant, making it an excellent choice for reforestation and sustainable development projects.

Chilean Forest Types & Representative Trees

Sclerophyllus	Espino, algarrobo, **peumo, quillay**, litre, maitén, **boldo**, molle, bollén, **northern belloto**.
Chilean Palm	**Chilean palm**, litre, **peumo, quillay**, espino, **boldo**, maitén.
Roble-hualo*	**Roble, hualo, raulí**, coihue, **cordilleran cypress, peumo**, lingue, **olivillo**, naranjillo, avellano, **boldo**, maitén, **ruil, quillay, laurel**, long-leaved mañio, **canelo, huala, tayú.**
Cordilleran Cypress	**Cordilleran cypress**, coihue, **roble, hualo, quillay, boldo**, litre, **peumo, olivillo, lingue, laurel**, long-leaved mañio, avellano, maitén, **lleque, huillipatagua.**
Roble-raulí-coihue*	**Roble, laurel, lingue**, ulmo, **olivillo**, coihue, tepa, long-leaved mañio, **raulí, queule, southern belloto, pitao, guindo santo, lleque.**
Lenga*	Lenga, coihue, **araucaria**, Magellanic coihue, **ñirre, raulí, roble, notro, radal, canelo**, Magellanic maitén.
Araucaria	**Araucaria**, lenga, coihue, **raulí, roble, ñirre.**
Coihue-raulí-tepa*	Coihue, **raulí**, tepa, **short-leaved mañio**, trevo, **tineo, olivillo, canelo**, ulmo, **prickly-leaved mañio**, meli.
Siempreverde*	Coihue, ulmo, tepa, **short-leaved mañio, tineo**, trevo, **canelo, olivillo**, luma, meli, Chiloé coihue, Magellanic coihue, **lingue**, avellano, **notro, prickly-leaved mañio**, long-leaved mañio, tiaca, **laurel**, myrceugenia.
Alerce	**Alerce**, coihue, Magallanic coihue, Chiloé coihue, **canelo, prickly-leaved mañio, short-leaved mañio**, Guaitecas cypress, tepa, **tineo**, arrayán, **notro, fuinque**, avellano, **radal**, tepú, **ñirre**, lenga, maitén.
Guaitecas cypress	Guaitecas cypress, Chiloé coihue, **prickly-leaved mañio**, Magallanic coihue, **ñirre, canelo**, avellano, **tineo**.
Magellanic coihue	Magallanic coihue, lenga, coihue, **canelo, notro**, Magellanic maitén, Guaitecas cypress, **sauco del diablo, prickly-leaved mañio, tineo, fuinque**.

* *Forest types supplying wood chips for export.*
Bold type = *Nationally and regionally listed endangered, vulnerable or rare species.*
Sources: CONAF, 1981, 1989; INFOR, 1990.

Forest Ecosystems in Chile

Matorral Espinoso Alto de Cauquenes
Bosque Caducifolio Andino del Bío-Bío
Bosque Caducifolio Interior
Bosque Esclerófilo de la Montaña
Bosque Caducifolio Alto-Andino de la Cordillera de Chillán
Matorrales Siempreverdes Oceánicos
Bosque Esclerófilo de los Arenales
Bosque Caducifolio Alto-Andino con Araucaria
Bosque Caducifolio del Llano
Bosque Caducifolio de la Montaña
Bosque Alto-Montaña de Nahuelbuta
Bosque Caducifolio Andino del Bío-Bío
Bosque Caducifolio Mixto de la Cordillera de los Andes
Bosque Caducifolio Maulino
Bosque Siempreverde/Turberas de los Chonos
Bosque Caducifolio de Concepción
Bosque Caducifolio de Valdivia
Matorrales Patagónicos con Araucaria
Bosque Caducifolio de la Frontera
Bosque Caducifolio de la Pre-Cordillera de Linares
Bosque Siempreverde Montano
Bosque Laurifolio de Valdivia
Bosque Laurifolio Andino
Bosque Laurifolio de los Lagos
Bosque Laurifolio de Chiloé
Bosque Siempreverde de la Cordillera de los Andes
Bosque Siempreverde de Puyuhuapi
Bosque Patagónico con Coníferas
Bosque Caducifolio Alto-Andino Húmedo
Bosque Caducifolio de Aisén
Mattorales Caducifolios Alto-Andino
Bosque Siempreverde de la Cordillera Pelada
Bosque Siempreverde/Turberas de la Isla Chiloé

Source: Gajardo, 1983.

Forests of Central Chile

 Sclerophyllus

 Cordilleran Cypress

 Coihue-Raulí-Tepa

 Chilean Palm

 Araucaria

 Roble-Hualo

 Roble-Raulí-Coihue

 Plantations

 Largely Deforested

 Non-Forested

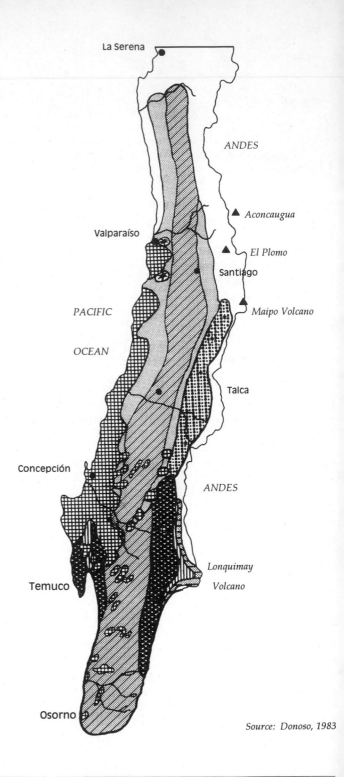

La Serena

ANDES

▲ Aconcaugua

Valparaíso

▲ El Plomo

Santiago

PACIFIC

▲ Maipo Volcano

OCEAN

Talca

Concepción

ANDES

Lonquimay
Volcano

Temuco

Osorno

Source: Donoso, 1983

1.1 Central Chile

THE FORESTS OF CENTRAL CHILE include virtually all the forested regions north of the Valdivian Rainforest. Crackling scrub and drought-tolerant trees lie scattered along the rim of the Atacama Desert 1,000 kilometers north of Santiago. In the northernmost reaches of lowland forest, stark barrens are cut by lush river corridors and oases fed by melting snow high in the Andes. The Atacama is the driest place on Earth, yet on a coastal mountain top in Fray Jorge National Park not far from La Serena, moist marine air rises up a steep escarpment and condenses into fog, providing a source of moisture sufficient to support a tiny rainforest—flanked on three sides by desert.

Nearer Santiago are lands that 500 years ago displayed a thick carpet of almost unbroken forest spilling from high mountain meadows downward into the great central valley, over the coastal ranges and out to the wild shores of the Pacific Ocean. Now, it is perhaps the most devastated bioregion in the nation. Productive farms and bustling cities dominate the once wooded landscape, while degraded and deforested land runs the length of the central valley, from the parched rim of the Atacama Desert well into the Lakes District, 600 kilometers south of the capital. Only the most remote parts, deep in the Andean and coastal cordilleras, remain relatively intact.

Of the seven major forest types in central Chile, most are in various stages of degradation. Millions of hectares of native forest have been lost or ruined by logging, agriculture and development, while more than 1.6 million are covered by pine and eucalyptus plantations, species that are not native to any part of South America. On the brighter side, substantial remnants of the seven forest types do exist, and efforts are underway to include representative portions of each in a national system of protected wildlands. (Two other forest types—lenga and *siempreverde*—are also found in central Chile; however, their primary range extends well to the south, merging with the Valdivian Rainforest. The lenga and *siempreverde*, or evergreen, forests are discussed in sections 1.2 and 1.3.)

Raulí

(*Nothofagus alpina*) is one of Chile's most valued commercial hardwood species. It is a large tree that reaches 40 meters in height and produces an excellent grade of wood used in furniture, cabinets and fine woodworking. Although not classified as rare or endangered, raulí has been heavily exploited throughout its range. A fast-growing tree, it is well suited to reforestation projects in south-central Chile.

Esclerófilo Forest *(Sclerophyllous)*

The northernmost trees of central Chile range within sight of the Atacama Desert and are adapted to very hot and dry conditions over much of the year. Trees are generally small, even shrub-like in size, and widely distributed throughout the central plain south of La Serena. The **esclerófilo**, or sclerophyllous, forest type is locally known as *espinales*, dominated by espino *(Acacia caven)* and other thorny trees with durable, water-conserving leaves.

The espinales are spread as far south as the Bío-Bío River where the mild Mediterranean climate lacks extremes in both temperature and rainfall. The natural range of the sclerophyllous forest roughly coincides with the first region in Chile to be invaded by the Spanish. The forest has since been burned, settled, cultivated, grazed, mined and industrialized: the first area in Chile to be substantially deforested. Only a few remnants of the original forest still stand, mostly against the foothills of the Andes and along the low range of coastal mountains to the west. Little has been protected outside La Campana National Park near Santiago.

What were once called espinales are now better known as *mattorales* or scrublands with little economic value to society. The trees that do regenerate in this ravaged and moderately populated region are quickly cut for firewood. In coastal areas, much of the sclerophyllous forest that existed five centuries ago is now plantation pine, largely devoid of any ecologic value to native flora and fauna.

Farther south, espino is less predominant, and other species like quillay, maitén, litre and boldo are more common. Northern and southern belloto, patagua, arrayán, pitra, peumo, lingue, naranjillo and canelo are typical of stream corridors, coasts and other humid places.

Palma Chilena (Chilean Palm)

Scattered among ravines and hollows in the esclerófilo forest are pockets of **Chilean palm** *(Jubaea chilensis)*, the southernmost palms in the world. They have long been exploited for their sweet syrup and nuts, and very few stands remain, mostly near Valparaíso. Now classified as a vulnerable species, these palms once ranged for several hundred miles to the north and south. The survivors now comprise the smallest of the twelve forest types in Chile.

Chilean Palm
Jubaea chilensis

Roble-Hualo Forest

A third forest type in central Chile is the **roble-hualo**, an open-canopy deciduous forest that is much more intact than the other forest types, though generally confined to a 200-mile stretch of the Andean foothills south of Santiago. The two dominant species that give the forest its name are well adapted to cooler temperatures and increased moisture, including snowy winters in the higher elevations. Roble *(Nothofagus obliqua)* and hualo *(N. glauca)* are also mixed with the sclerophyllous forest in transition areas on the lower slopes. A similar forest once existed in the coastal range as well, but pine plantations have essentially displaced it.

Some of the more important tree species associated with this forest type are peumo, litre, boldo, maitén, quillay, huala (a natural hybrid between roble and hualo), and in wet places coihue, laurel, olivillo and canelo. Under the right soil and microclimate conditions, pure stands of roble or hualo are known to occur. Both can reach great size and have been extensively harvested in the past for lumber.

The northern reaches of the forest became so devoid of accessible timber that as early as 1900 roble, raulí, coihue and araucaria logs, among others, were shipped from the south to population centers around Santiago. The price of raulí is reported to have increased five-fold from 1900 to 1910. Ruil, another large tree associated with the roble-hualo forest, was also severely exploited. This rarest member of the southern beech family is now recognized as an endangered species, although it has not been specifically protected by law.

In the lower valleys to the south, the roble-hualo forest often occupies fertile, well-drained soils suitable for agriculture. Roble, therefore, has been looked to by *campesinos* as a kind of indicator species signifying good soils for farming. The tree actually grows in some of the best *and* worst soils in central Chile. The result: substantial areas of old-growth roble have been cleared over the last hundred years only to expose soils that are hopeless for cultivation — and not much better for livestock. Recovery of these once-productive forests is an important component of potential sustainable development projects in south-central Chile.

Hualo
(Nothofagus glauca) and Huala (*N. leonii*, a natural hybrid between hualo and roble) are both large trees when mature, although most have been destroyed. Accordingly, they are classified as <u>vulnerable</u> to extinction. Hualo produces a fine lumber and could be grown commercially in mixed stands.

Cordilleran Cypress

(Austrocedrus chilensis), one of only eight large conifers native to Chile, grows at moderate elevations in the Andes. The wood is very strong and resists decay, making it ideal for exterior construction—attributes that also help explain its demise. It is considered a vulnerable species.

Pitao

(Pitavia punctata) is another endangered tree severely impacted by centuries of development and agricultural activity. It is a densely foliated broadleaf evergreen that is both fragrant and attractive. Pitao is an endemic species found only along the coast.

Ciprés de la Cordillera *(Cordilleran Cypress)*

In the same region as the roble-hualo forest, but generally limited to warm, dry, rocky and exposed sites, **ciprés de la cordillera** or cordilleran cypress *(Austrocedrus chilensis)* comprises the second-smallest forest type in central Chile. Its range extends east and southward into Argentina as well.

The conical-shaped cordilleran cypress inhabits difficult, often volcanic sites that other species in adjacent habitats cannot tolerate. As a result, this unique conifer tends to occur in small pure stands that can thrive for centuries.

Roble-Raulí-Coihue Forest

The **roble-raulí-coihue** forest type is unusual in that it did not develop naturally in central Chile. It is a largely degraded second-growth forest comprised of many species but with few mature individuals. Chileans more commonly refer to this forest as *los renovales*. Large-scale cutting and burning for agriculture and development and the introduction of domestic animals are responsible for the degradation of this once pristine landscape.

The three dominant trees that give the forest its name are southern beech species (*N. obliqua, N. alpina* and *N. dombeyi*) and they are the most aggressive trees to grow in these regions. Each is adapted to the area's soil and climate conditions and each can grow rapidly under a relatively open canopy. They are intolerant of shade which makes it difficult for seedlings to survive. Regeneration, therefore, is stifled. All three can be found in both pure and mixed stands, although coihue tends to inhabit the higher elevations while roble stays low. The *renovales* occupy a broad band of lowland valleys and foothills from 36° to 40° S, reaching well into the Lakes District. The forest rises to 1,000 meters in both the Andean and coastal cordilleras.[9] About 600,000 hectares are thought to exist.[10]

Originally, these forests were comprised of roble, laurel and lingue as dominants in much more complex ecosystems than what exists today. Ulmo, olivillo and avellano were also common in the lower elevations, while tepa, trevo, mañío and lenga became more frequent with altitude. A few remnants of the original forest still stand and efforts are underway to protect them. As for the rest, with careful management, the *renovales* could become a truly renewed and productive ecosystem of high environmental and economic value. The roble-raulí-coihue forest is an ideal environment in which to develop models for sustainable forestry in Chile.[11]

Coihue-Raulí-Tepa Forest

Inhabiting the same general region of Chile as the roble-raulí-coihue forest, but at moderate elevations in both mountain ranges, is the **coihue-raulí-tepa** forest. Degraded areas are much like the *renovales* described above. At the higher elevations, the forest often merges with lenga and araucaria.

Southern parts of the forest experience abundant rainfall, contributing to the development of the rich communities of plants typical of the *siempreverde*, or evergreen, rainforest. Raulí, however, becomes quite scarce south toward the *siempreverde*. The forest is comprised of an interesting mix of deciduous and evergreen species. Other important species in this forest type are short-leaved mañio, trevo, tineo and olivillo.

All three dominants (*N. dombeyi, N. alpina* and *Laureliopsis phillippiana*) produce high-quality wood fiber. Raulí is an exceptionally fast-growing native species and holds great promise for ecosystem-based forestry projects in south-central Chile.

Roble (Nothofagus obliqua)
❀ Adriana Hoffmann

Raulí (Nothofagus alpina)
❀ Adriana Hoffmann

Araucaria Forest

One of the most spectacular forests in the world is Chile's renowned **araucaria forest**. The tree's tall spindly trunk and unusual evergreen foliage give it a distinct form that can be recognized from a distance of several kilometers. Fabulous scenes of ancient araucaria (*Araucaria araucana*) jutting from the crest of a distant volcanic ridge are unforgettable.

The forest occurs in two areas of Chile at high elevations: above 900 meters in the Andes between 37° and 40° S; and above 1,000 meters at 37-38° S in the coastal range of Nahuelbuta. Perhaps 300,000 hectares of forest still contain araucaria, including about 50,000 hectares in pure stands (the other 250,000 may contain as little as one araucaria tree per hectare).[12] Araucaria thrives in the region's temperate climate with its warm dry summers and cold snowy winters. The understory is relatively open in most areas. However, in the southern reach of the tree's Andean range, the forest is deluged by more than four meters of annual rainfall, producing a most dramatic display of temperate rainforest. At Nahuelbuta in the north, fog is a major source of moisture.

Because it frequently grows in pure stands, araucaria is typically the only dominant species. Lenga and ñirre are commonly encountered in natural breaks and coihue often inhabits disturbed areas within the forest. Roble, ulmo, tineo, laurel, and occasionally raulí are associated with araucaria as well. Quila or bamboo (*Chusquea quila*) and michay (*Berberis spp.*) are common in the forest understory.

Araucaria is a slow-growing tree that has been severely exploited for the high-grade lumber it produces. The yellow wood was used for flooring, veneer, truck bodies, pulp, mining timbers and general construction lumber. A century ago, its cylindrical and

Araucaria

Araucaria araucana) is an elegant tree, predominant in its range. It is typically found at high elevations in the Andes and the central coastal range at Nahuelbuta. The tree grows to 50 meters in height, more than three meters in diameter and may exceed 2,000 years of age (second only to the alerce in Chile).

Like the cordilleran cypress, araucaria is often found in pure stands in volcanic terrain. It is adapted to summer drought, torrential rains, and winter wind and snow. Very thick bark makes the tree resistant to damage by fire or extreme cold. It has a long history of commercial exploitation and has been classified as a species <u>vulnerable</u> to extinction.

The umbrella canopy of the araucaria forest is distinctive.

❀ Dan Dancer

uniform trunk was prized as an excellent mast for sailing ships. When the first *Araucaria araucana* was delivered to an English nurseryman in the 1800s, he remarked what a puzzle it would be for a monkey to climb; thus, the name Europeans and North Americans are more accustomed to. Its stiff and prickly branches swirl around the trunk, impenetrable, and often in the classic form of an umbrella. There are, however, no monkeys in Chile to attempt the climb, so the name has no relevance to the tree's ecology.

The Spanish named the tree in the 17th century for the land they called Araucanía, in the region of the Bío-Bío River. They called all the native people of this region "Araucanians" — instead of the unique names these people gave themselves. Two principal surviving groups are the *Mapuche* (People of the Land) and the *Pehuenche* (People of the Pehuen). *Pehuen* means araucaria.

Today, botanists recognize the araucaria as an "archetypal" tree, among the earliest families of seed-bearing trees ever produced in nature. As the great swamp-forests of the Carboniferous period began to recede a quarter of a billion years ago (long before the dinosaurs appeared), the first pines were reaching out to drier ground. Few species had evolved that could tolerate the poor soils and occasional droughts that occurred outside the coastal swamps.

The fossilized remains of *Araucarioxylon*, early ancestor of the

Left to right: Mature pehuen (araucaria) tree ready for harvest; Pehuenche family collecting piñones at Quinquen; tree trunk and thick, fire-resistant bark.
❀ Harold Schlange
❀ Ken Wilcox

araucaria, are scattered across the desert in Argentine Patagonia and at Petrified Forest National Monument in Arizona. About twenty species of araucaria survive in the world today. From the time the fossils of *Araucarioxylon* were first laid down, the araucaria family has proved to be one of nature's most successful innovations — 200,000,000 years old and counting.

In summer, the large female cones in the top-most branches of the tree produce clusters of 200 or more inch-and-a-half-long pine nuts called "piñones." They are the staple of the Pehuenche people who inhabit the forests and meadows of this high, volcanic region. Each seed is a hard, creamy-white fruit firmly wrapped in a papery husk. The cones, or fruit balls, are as big as pineapples and fall or are knocked to the ground when ripe in mid- to late-summer. They are collected, dried and stored for year-round consumption.

Piñones are eaten fresh-roasted, boiled, or dried (usually on a hot tin roof) and ground into flour or meal that can be used in a variety of delightful concoctions. After they have been cooked a few minutes, one simply pinches the fatter end of the husk and the seed pops out, sweet and steaming. Nutritional values are considered very high.

The araucaria survives in much lower numbers today than in the past. For more than a century, its high-quality wood was severely exploited by non-natives. Accelerated cutting of both araucaria and alerce in the 1970s was rejected by a concerned public and the military government was persuaded to prohibit further cutting in 1976. The araucaria species was immediately declared a Natural Monument.

The government lifted the ban in 1987 and the species' tiny

range shrunk even more until President Aylwin restored its Monument status within weeks of his inauguration in 1990. Felling of this sacred "mother tree" of the Pehuenche, and what Chileans revere as their national tree is prohibited once again.

Of the remaining 300,000 hectares of forest containing araucaria, three-fourths is located on private land. Nearly all of the publicly owned forest is protected as parks and reserves. However, this is well short of what is needed to ensure the health and genetic variability of the species and the long-term viability of the ecosystem. Natural and human-caused calamities have destroyed forests by the hundreds of thousands of hectares. Faced with future disasters and lacking a large block of surviving forest, recovery could be exceedingly difficult.

Preservation efforts are ongoing for the benefit of this unique forest. The Cañi Forest Sanctuary, a project sponsored by Ancient Forest International and the Lahuen Foundation, offers a creative example of what can be done to safeguard a private araucaria forest. *[See photo on page 82.]*

Despite these efforts and the protections emplaced by the government, timber companies continue to lobby for a return to the legal harvest of araucaria forests.

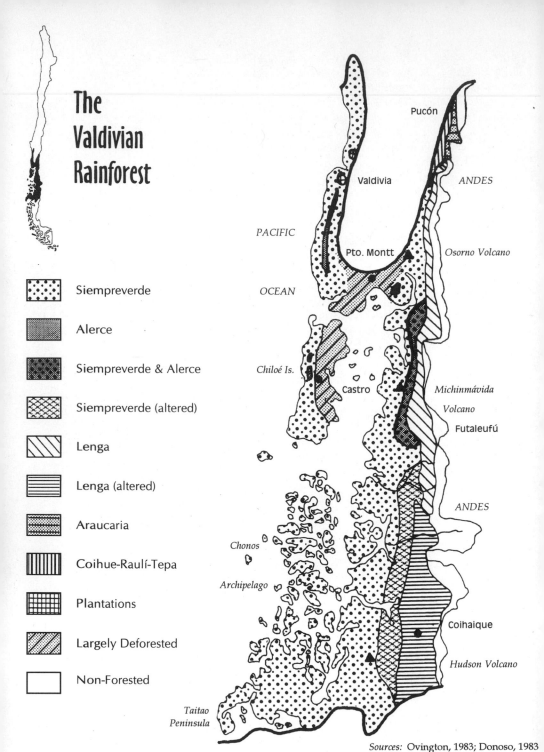

The Valdivian Rainforest

Pucón

Valdivia

ANDES

PACIFIC

Pto. Montt

Osorno Volcano

OCEAN

Chiloé Is.

Castro

Michinmávida
Volcano

Futaleufú

ANDES

Chonos

Archipelago

Coihaique

Hudson Volcano

Taitao
Peninsula

Legend:
- Siempreverde
- Alerce
- Siempreverde & Alerce
- Siempreverde (altered)
- Lenga
- Lenga (altered)
- Araucaria
- Coihue-Raulí-Tepa
- Plantations
- Largely Deforested
- Non-Forested

Sources: Ovington, 1983; Donoso, 1983

1.2 The Valdivian Rainforest

MOST OF THE REMAINING NATIVE FOREST outside central Chile exists in the form of a great *coastal temperate rainforest*—the world's second-largest. Only the Pacific Northwest coastal rainforest bioregion (from northern California to southeast Alaska) covers more land area. Unlike the Northwest, Chile's rainforest is mostly comprised of broadleaf evergreens instead of conifers. Similar rainforests are also found in Tasmania and on South Island, New Zealand. In both hemispheres all temperate rainforests add up to barely 30 million hectares.[13] That is just a tiny fraction—less than three percent—of the much more widespread rainforests of the tropics.

Tropical rainforests are well known for their sprawling (albeit shrinking) size and incredible diversity of species; however, scientists now recognize their cooler counterparts in the temperate latitudes as among the oldest, most resilient and productive ecosystems on Earth. Additionally, temperate rainforests contain far more biomass per hectare—up to a thousand metric tons in Chile—than does an equivalent area of tropical rainforest.[14]

In Chile there are, more or less, three identifiable regions of temperate rainforest: the Valdivian, North Patagonian, and Magellanic Rainforests.[15] Together they comprise about 7.6 million hectares or nearly one-quarter of all temperate rainforests on the planet.[16] The northerly of the three, the Valdivian, is named for a beautiful, centuries-old city originally built by Pedro de Valdivia, founder of Chile and a former officer under Francisco Pizarro, conqueror of the Incas.

The Valdivian Rainforest is a rich and tangled forest, drenched in winter, a little less wet in summer. Annual rainfall averages two and half meters at Valdivia, increasing to more than five meters (about 16 feet) in the higher elevations. The standing forest today accounts for a large share of Chile's rainforest, yet no one knows exactly how much. It is also uncertain how much of the Valdivian Rainforest has been destroyed, although it is surely in the millions of hectares.

Coihue

(Nothofagus dombeyi), the largest broadleaf tree in Chile, can live for a millennium. At lower elevations the tree reaches 50 meters in height and its huge gray trunk can grow to four meters in diameter. Its branches and leaves have a distinct stratified appearance, making it one of Chile's most attractive broadleaf species.

Although heavily exploited for lumber and fuelwood for more than a century, it is still considered abundant in the south. A climax evergreen species, most coihue was burned prior to the 1950s. It was so abundant at the time that it had little market value. Today, the smooth-grained wood is used in heavy construction, plywood, boats, railroad ties and piers. Coihue ranges from 35° to 45° S and tends to occupy damp sites from sea level to timberline.

Ulmo

(Eucryphia cordifolia) is a lovely summer-blooming tree of the south, famous for the sweet ulmo honey produced by bees. Conspicuous white blossoms of this large and abundant tree add a lively contrast to the dark green depths of the coastal rainforest. The fine-grained wood is mostly valued for heavy construction and for firewood, although the wood has also been used for truck bodies, particle board and plywood. Ulmo is found from 37° to 43° S especially in coastal mountains on damp sites from sea level to 700 meters. It often grows with coihue, tepa and roble.

The Chilean rainforest began to form (or possibly reform) following the retreat of continental glaciers more than 10,000 years ago. Evidence suggests that as the forest developed, the cool and relatively dry climate became much more humid as it warmed.[17] The changing climate was perpetuated, at least in part, by the effects of evapotranspiration within the forest itself. By about 6,500 years ago, the lush, closed-canopy environment we see today was fully established, and persisted quite satisfactorily for the next 6,400 years. For millennia, the plant species that inhabit the region have remained essentially unchanged.

The Valdivian Rainforest has no clear boundaries. The heart of the forest could be described as an area that generally coincides with the *siempreverde* (evergreen) and alerce forest types. However, by some definitions, a much more extensive area could be included that is loosely comprised of at least seven broad forest types. *Siempreverde* is the predominant form. The other six are alerce, lenga, araucaria, roble-raulí-coihue, coihue-raulí-tepa and Magellanic coihue. All or part of each forest type is subject to a relatively high rate of annual rainfall. There are exceptions, of course. Microclimates, human disturbances and other factors exist which may persuade an ecologist who relies on a strict rainforest definition to include or exclude certain areas.

Paul Alaback, a forest ecologist with the U.S. Forest Service in Juneau, Alaska, has written about the temperate rainforests of Chile and the Pacific Northwest and has suggested a technical definition for temperate rainforest climatic zones.[18] He offers the following:

- *>1,400 mm annual rainfall; >10% in summer*
- *<16° C. mean temperature during the warmest month*
- *Frequent summer overcast*
- *Infrequent fires*
- *Winter dormancy in plants*

Portions of all seven forest types listed above are likely to satisfy these parameters, despite the exceptions. Osorno, for example, is about 100 kilometers south of Valdivia, but receives only half as much rain due to a rainshadow effect of the coastal mountains. Rainforest may be absent or less developed as a result. On the other hand, wetter portions of adjoining forest types, such as the araucaria or lenga forest, ought to be included. As the science of temperate rainforest ecology — still in its infancy in both hemispheres — advances, boundaries and definitions should become clearer.

In the lowlands, predominant rainforest trees include several southern beech *(Nothofagus)* species, mañio *(Podocarpus)* and a variety of associated broadleaf evergreens. Above 500 meters in elevation are lenga, araucaria and alerce. Alerce, a magnificent Chilean cypress, is the most abundant conifer in the higher elevations of the rainforest. These communities constitute some of the highest concentrations of biomass of any ecosystem in the world.[19]

In all seven forest types represented in the Valdivian Rainforest, large areas have been disturbed or destroyed as a result of logging, agriculture and development. Around the turn of the century, the shipbuilding and railroad industries consumed vast amounts of native forest timber. Today, clearcut logging and substitution for non-native plantations, high-grading for chips, land-clearing, and collection of fuelwood are major factors in the continuing devastation of native forests in the rainforest region. Although plantation forestry was much less developed here just a few years ago, the conversion of natural forest to pine and eucalyptus has increased rapidly in the 1990s, particularly in the northern reaches of the rainforest nearer Valdivia.

Species diversity and the overall production of biomass in the Valdivian Rainforest are nearly as great as that of the high-latitude rainforests of the Pacific Northwest, including the classic spruce-hemlock forests of British Columbia and the Olympic Mountains of Washington state. The richest and most abundant of all Chilean forest types, the *siempreverde* or literally "forevergreen" forest, is a place that Chile's Nobel Prize-winning poet, Pablo Neruda, wrote so fondly of in his famous works on nature, people and politics.

Of the forest types occurring within the Valdivian Rainforest region, only the *siempreverde* and alerce are discussed in this

Luma

(Amomyrtus luma) is an attractive and very fragrant evergreen tree that grows to 30 meters in height and is common to the Valdivian Rainforest. The tree is shade-tolerant and grows very slowly. It produces edible berries and a wood that is extremely hard and resistant to decay. Luma has been used for tool handles, posts and police clubs. In the rainforest, it forms an important component of the sub-canopy.

"Anyone who hasn't been in the Chilean forest doesn't know this planet..."
Pablo Neruda,
Memoirs [1977]

section. Refer to the previous section for descriptions of araucaria, roble-raulí-coihue and coihue-raulí-tepa forest types. Lenga and Magallanic coihue are discussed in the section on the Far South.

It should be emphasized that these forest types were developed by CONAF for forest management purposes rather than for purely ecological reasons. Other more technical classifications by Gajardo (1983) or Veblen, Schlegel & Oltremari (1980) provide much more detail— more than can be expounded here. The CONAF system was considered most useful for this overview.

As we increase our knowledge and refine the classification of Chile's native forests in coming years, the expertise and observations of both foresters and forest ecologists should become more readily available to people concerned about the forest.

Canelo

(Drimys winteri) is a hardwood tree typical of the Chiloé region and sacred to the Mapuches. It grows rapidly and is tolerant of both shade and full sunlight but is vulnerable to drought. Canelo is the only hardwood that, like conifers, has no pores.

Ranging between 30° and 56° S, most canelo is found in Region X, where there are dense stands. Its cylindrical trunks can reach a meter across and the tree can grow to 30 meters high. It occurs in pure stands or mixed with tepa, coihue, mañio and Guaitecas cypress. The wood is used in particle board, furniture, carving and general applications, making it an economically viable species for restoration, especially in wet areas.

Siempreverde Forest *(Evergreen)*

The forest type with the richest diversity in Chile is the *siempreverde* or evergreen forest. It is the major component of the Valdivian and North Patagonian Rainforests and is one of the more complex and widespread forest types of southern Chile. The *siempreverde* extends from about 47° S at the Península de Taitao north through the Chonos Archipelago, Chiloé and the coastal cordillera to about 38° S (northwest of Temuco). In the Andes, the forest extends only as far north as 40° S (almost due east of Valdivia). It is a lowland forest, particularly in the Andes where it seldom rises above 1,000 meters above sea level.[20]

In the north, this forest mixes with the roble-raulí-coihue and coihue-raulí-tepa forest types and becomes hard to distinguish from the others. Along the edges of the central plain, the forest merges with remnants of the roble-laurel-lingue forest type. Near Puerto Montt, a *siempreverde-alerce* forest once occupied a large basin north of Reloncaví Sound and the Gulf of Ancud but was virtually destroyed by German colonists in the late 1800s. In the higher Andean elevations, the *siempreverde* merges with lenga and alerce forests, and with Magellanic coihue in the far south.

Throughout the *siempreverde*, the dominant species vary from one location to the next. In fact, the *siempreverde* is really a wide range of forest communities often comprised of four or five layers or canopies of vegetation and differing combinations of broadleaf evergreen dominants. As a result, a number of sub-types have been identified.[21] Overall, floral composition seems to change with latitude and altitude as well as with slope aspect, climate, soil and drainage characteristics.

Some of the more common tree species encountered in the *siempreverde* include coihue, ulmo, tineo, tepa, luma, canelo and tiaca. Common shrubs like quila (bamboo), tepú *(Tepualia stipularis)* and picha *(Myrceugenia planipes)* can form dense, if not impenetrable, thickets beneath a canopy of tall trees covered with epiphytes and climbing plants. Several bromeliads (orchid relatives) are frequently seen clinging to the trunks of trees. Canelilla *(Hydrangea serratifolia)*, a giant rainforest hydrangea, is Chile's largest creeper. Its thick foliage and stem (up to 35 cm in diameter) can completely engulf trees 40 meters tall, doing a good deal of harm in the process. Quila is so abundant on the forest floor that it can impact the regeneration and composition of the forest.[22] South America's tallest moss also thrives in the *siempreverde*.

Prickly-Leaved Mañio

(Podocarpus nubigena) is one of the few conifers of the lower elevation rainforest. It occurs from 39° to 48° S latitude in wet or swampy soils close to streams and water bodies and is most common in the coastal range. A mature tree trunk can reach two meters across and is free of branches for most of its 25-meter height. Mañio is often found mixed with tepa, canelo, coihue and alerce. The wood is similar to the pine that grows in Nordic countries and has been used for flooring, windows, veneer, plywood, crates, masts, oars, rudders and decks.

A sleek stand of arrayán trees, one of the more attractive broadleaf evergreens of the siempreverde forest.
❀ Peter McBride

Alerce

(Fitzroya cupressoides) is the classic monarch of the ancient forests in Chile. It is the oldest and, at four-plus meters in diameter, among the largest known trees of the southern hemisphere. An extremely slow-growing tree, a typical alerce is barely a meter in diameter by the time it reaches 1,000 years of age. The tree is known to exceed 3,600 years[23] and ecologists suggest that some individuals may reach 4,000 years or more.

Like the coast redwood and red cedar of the Pacific Northwest, alerce produces a straight-grained, rot-resistant, reddish-brown fiber with very thin rings. The wood is easy to work and has been widely used for split shakes and shingles.

Alerce grows in a cool, rainy environment from 39° to 43° S in the higher elevations of the Andean and coastal cordilleras, including the great island of Chiloé. In the upper reaches of the Valdivian Rainforest, alerce is often associated with coihue and lenga although it frequently occurs in pure, majestic stands. Alerce is protected as a Natural Monument.

In coastal areas, Chiloé coihue and Magellanic coihue tend to replace common coihue *(N. dombeyi)* in the southernmost regions of the forest where the evergreen avellano *(Gevuina avellana)* disappears altogether. Olivillo and prickly-leaved mañío ("hojas punzantes") are common to the south and near the coast while short-leaved mañío ("hojas cortas") is more prevalent in the Andes. A rich variety of fungi, mosses, ferns and flowering herbs, including the endangered copihue, Chile's national flower, complete the predominant floral mosaic of the *siempreverde*.

Alerce Forest

Hidden in remote valleys, slopes, and terraces of the higher elevations of southern Chile (normally above 700 meters) are the last remnants of ancient **alerce forest**. The giant alerece *(Fitzroya cupressoides)* are among the oldest and largest trees in the southern hemisphere. *Norteamericanos* may notice a resemblance to the coast redwoods of California, though alerce is not nearly as tall. It is a <u>vulnerable</u> species that lives in pure, towering stands or in the company of *Nothofagus* evergreens. Like the redwoods, the alerce forest has a long history of exploitation.

The stands that remain are discontinuous and largely inaccessible in the Andes from 40° to 44° S, and in the coastal mountains and on the island of Chiloé from 39° to 42.5° S. High rainfall and humidity over much of the year have sustained this ecosystem — and individual trees — for millennia. Trees more than 3,600 years old and 4.5 meters in diameter are known; mammoths 4,000 years old and 5 meters across are highly probable.

Alerce has not always been restricted to the remote high country. Decaying stumps and perhaps a few isolated survivors of a lowland variety of alerce near Puerto Montt are all that remain of an extensive cathedral forest that was burned and cleared a century ago. Today farms, wetlands and poorly drained fields of scrub vegetation mark this severely disturbed landscape or *ñadi* as it is known in Chile. A shallow layer of hardpan contributes to the problem. Where forest does survive, it is dominated by coihue and canelo.

In the coastal range, alerce is generally associated with Chiloé coihue, prickly-leaved mañío, tineo and Guaitecas cypress. The intermediate canopy may be comprised of smaller trees like ñirre, arrayán, and fuinque, with quila dominant among shrubs. Alerce disappears as the forest blends into the *siempreverde* at lower elevations. In the Andes, coihue, canelo, prickly-leaved and short-leaved mañíos, tepa and Magellanic and Chiloé coihues are the most important trees in the alerce-dominated forest. A vibrant understory of quila, dwarf canelo, taique, Magellanic maitén, sev-

Alerce forest, trees estimated at 2,000-3,000 years old.   ❀ Douglas Fir

eral varieties of heath and barberry, and a host of colorful herbs and ferns including an abundance of epiphytes are also present.

The future outlook for alerce forest is hopeful, but tenuous. Large-scale destruction of alerce ceased in 1976 following a supreme decree of the president. This victory for the forest was a milestone in Chilean environmentalism. A good deal of the credit goes to the National Committee for the Defense of Fauna and Flora, or CODEFF, a highly respected organization of environmental experts and activists who confronted head-on what some regarded as a stoutly anti-environment regime. After thousands of hectares of alerce forest had been clearcut by Chilean and North American timber companies, strong public opposition to the cutting led to a ban on any further exploitation of live trees. Exports were prohibited and the alerce was protected internationally with a listing in the Convention on International Trade in Endangered Species (CITES, Appendix 1).[24] In Chile, the tree was designated a Natural Monument.

Despite the ban, some poaching of live alerce still occurs on a regular basis, and many more trees are killed by fire or deliberate stripping of their protective bark. Dead alerce can be collected legally, and every accessible downed tree is cut into manageable timbers by hard-working *alerceros* who cart them off to the nearest community to be sold as lumber or hand-split shingles.

Olivillo

(Aextoxicon punctatum) is an abundant hardwood that grows on rainforest slopes below the alerce, ranging from 35° to 44° S. Its straight, cylindrical trunk reaches a meter across and an overall height of 25 meters. Olivillo associates with roble, coihue, ulmo, tepa and tineo but is often found in pure stands on the southern coast. The wood is used for windows, trim, furniture, plywood, doors, floors and barrel staves.

Tepa

(Laureliopsis philippiana), a large, abundant evergreen, can grow to 30 meters high in the Valdivian Rainforest. Its range extends from 37° to 47° S and to 500 meters above sea level. Tepa is similar to laurel but often associates with coihue, tineo, ulmo, canelo, mañio and olivillo. The wood is hard and has a fine texture that is highly valued for furniture, plywood, moldings, doors, planks, and carvings.

Parque Pumalin

As much as 35% of all remaining alerce can be found on 270,000 hectares of Chilean rainforest recently acquired by Doug Tompkins, American businessman, and benefactor of the Foundation for Deep Ecology and, in Chile, the Foundation for Education, Science, and Ecology. Once transactions are completed, the area will become *Parque Pumalin*, a world-class reserve and park *(photos p.30,124)*.

The alerce is truly one of the world's most magnificent forests. The lowland subspecies *(mentioned above)* that was dominant in a part of the Valdivian Rainforest that stretched across the central plain from Puerto Varas to Puerto Montt at the northern edge of the Chilean fiords, can hardly be imagined. The largest trees in Chile, three to five meters across and thousands of years old, grew here until the entire forest, an estimated 27,500 hectares, was burned to obliteration in the late 1800s in order to clear the land for farms.[25] Regrettably, poor soils, shallow hardpan conditions, and miserable drainage rendered much of the land unsuitable for cultivation. It remains, to this day, a swampy, stump-filled wasteland of little ecologic or economic value.

Of the higher elevation alerce forests that do remain, representative ecosystems are contained in several national parks and reserves, notably Alerce Andino, Vincente Pérez Rosales and Chiloé National Parks, and in Hornopirén and Alerce Costero Natural Monuments. There is concern, still, that existing protected areas are inadequate to ensure the long-term viability of the forest. CODEFF has taken the lead on alerce forest preservation efforts since the 1970s and it remains a high priority nationwide.

On another front, Ancient Forest International has co-sponsored with Chilean participants several research and photographic excursions into the rarely explored fiord region of southern Chile in an effort to determine the quality and extent of the remaining alerce stands. Working with CODEFF, Fundación Lahuen, Bosque Antiguo and other Chilean organizations, AFI has, since 1988, strived to bring the plight of one of the world's most ancient forest ecosystems to the attention of the international environmental community. As a result, alerce forests have become widely recognized as a globally unique and endangered.

Still, the future of the alerce forest remains uncertain. Large-scale clearing activity in the past combined with very slow growth, poor regeneration, and illegal cutting will seriously impede any notable increase in the natural distribution of alerce for the foreseeable future.

Finally, there is a brighter picture in all of this that cannot be overlooked. Through foundation support, the cooperation of conscientious land-owners, and the generosity of individuals, large areas of alerce and southern beech rainforest have been acquired privately since 1990 for park or preservation purposes.[26] Doug Tompkins, a tireless friend of Chile's temperate rainforests (as well as AFI's work in Chile), has purchased 270,000 hectares of wildlands in the northern fiord region to become "Parque Pumalin" *(see sidebar)*. Tompkins work has been a huge undertaking, immersed in complexity and politics, yet fully consistent with Chile's new Law of Private Parks (1994). This laudable effort is unique in the world and clearly deserves everyone's support.

Non-Native Trees in Chile

"Alien" tree species introduced to central and southern Chile include...

Monterey pine (*Pinus radiata*), presently the most economically valuable species in Chile. The tree was introduced from California and Mexico nearly a century ago. Widely planted in Chile, it ranges from 33° S to Region X in both the central valley and coastal ranges. Monterey pine grows rapidly and can reach 50 meters in height and a meter in diameter, producing attractive, knot-free wood for lumber as well as supplying the massive wood chip and pulp industries. Well over a million hectares have been planted since 1974, with as many as 60,000 hectares or more added annually, which is about two-thirds of all areas planted (or replanted) each year.

Eucalyptus (*Eucalyptus viminalis, E. regnans, E delegatensis, etc.*), grown commercially in Chile for decades (mostly *E. globulus*). Under the right conditions it grows faster than pine. A native to eastern Australia and Tasmania, eucalyptus has been planted in Chile between 29° and 39° S and from the Pacific coast to 400 meters above sea level. Its straight, cylindrical trunk is free of branches and towers to 60 meters in height. (Old-growth eucalyptus in Tasmania approaches 100 meters, making it the world's tallest known broadleaf tree.) The tree produces a heavy hardwood that is difficult to work, but useful in heavy construction, flooring, veneers, pulp, furniture, railroad ties, utility poles and charcoal. It is notorious for causing serious wear and tear on saws. Eucalyptus resists fungi, dries poorly and easily splits and cracks. Nevertheless, the wood burns very well and may play an important role in producing large volumes of fuelwood in as little as ten-year rotations, thus helping to reduce the Chilean woodcutters' impact on native forests. About 240,000 hectares of eucalyptus have been planted in Chile.

Alamo (*Populus spp.*), imported from Europe and Asia. In Chile all species are grouped under the name "black poplar." They are commonly seen as wind breaks along property boundaries, roads and lanes, or as plantations (*P. euroamericana*). Alamo is most common in the central valley from 33° to 45° S. It is used commercially for ice cream sticks, match sticks, chopsticks and utility planking.

Douglas fir (*Pseudotsuga menziesii*), another fast-growing tree introduced to Chile from the Pacific Northwest. Although it cannot compete with pine in terms of annual growth, over 12,000 hectares of plantations have been established. It is generally found between 35° and 43° S, to 1,800 meters in elevation, often in acid soils. The tree grows 60 meters high and two meters in diameter. The wood is used in laminates, lumber, plywood, furniture and shipbuilding.

Seven thousand miles northwest of the Valdivian Rainforest, are people who live, work and recreate in the ancient rainforests of the Pacific Northwest. Many Northwesterners would feel right at home in the cool evergreen forests of Southern Chile. In both regions, forest ecosystems have developed in a cool, wet climate stirred by marine air rolling in from the Pacific Ocean.

The wild, mountainous landscapes of the two coasts are remarkably alike, cut by rivers of water and ice, crowned by volcanoes and cloaked in rainforest. Rain, fog, wind and shade produce difficult growing conditions in both regions that only a select number of trees can tolerate. The forests share many important ecological characteristics as a result.

Some of the younger evergreen *Nothofagus* species, for example, will grow very slowly under a full canopy, then shoot up quickly once an opening occurs — much like silver fir in the Pacific Northwest. Both forests depend on natural disturbances to create gaps in the canopy. Low-elevation coihue, roble and rauli, like Sitka spruce, often depend on catastrophic disturbances for regeneration: floods, landslides, fire, volcanic ash, wind storms.

One unusual, albeit widespread southern beech tree, lenga, often grows in heavy snowpack areas above the true rainforest, a characteristic shared by mountain hemlock in the Pacific Northwest. Alerce and coihue, like western red cedar and coast redwood, contain resins that resist decomposition, making them especially valuable woods for exterior construction.

Many broadleaf trees including most *Nothofagus* species tend to be shade-intolerant, yet they are abundant in both humid and dry forests. Shade-intolerant conifers include cordilleran cypress, Guaiteca cypress and alerce. Alerce, like Douglas fir, requires a mineral seed bed for germination since the tiny seed roots cannot penetrate the duff and debris that build on the forest floor. Douglas fir frequently relies on fire to expose the soil; alerce depends on landslides. Shade-tolerant conifers in Chile include prickly-leaved and short-leaved mañios. Semi-tolerant species are lleuque, long-leaved mañio and araucaria. Western hemlock and Sitka spruce are good examples of shade-tolerant species in the Northwest. Fog is an important source of water for some forests, particularly in the north coastal areas (Fray Jorge National Park near La Serena is

Lush ferns thrive in both regions. ❀ Peter McBride

High in the southern Andes. ❀ Ken Wilcox

a prime example). In the northern hemisphere, the redwoods form a classic "fog-forest" along the coast of northern California, where fog can amount to the equivalent of ten inches of rain or more over the growing season. (One of the most biologically dramatic fog-dependent ecosystems on Earth is Chile's "Paposo," a rich, treeless, coastal desert to the north, below Antofagasta. It is comprised mostly of endemic species, many of them classified as rare or endangered. A new species was discovered there in 1991 that was so unusual botanists were unable to place it in any known family of plants.[27] Currently owned by a mining company, Paposo is CONAF's #1 priority for preservation nationwide. Unfortunately, funds have not been available for acquisition.)

Old-growth or "late successional" forests in both hemispheres are impressive stores of biomass and biodiversity. Yet, we understand little about the real contributions these ecosystems make to the health of the global environment. They are vast stores of carbon that, when released by fire or decay, serve to warm our atmosphere. Left alone by humanity, production and mortality tend to balance out and stored carbon remains more or less constant. Natural cycling of nutrients continues uninterrupted, species interact, and life persists in much the same way it has for thousands, even millions, of years. Biological diversity remains rich and dynamic over time. We call these natural balancing acts "equilibrium" and perhaps nowhere else on the planet is the phenomenon better expressed than in the wildest remaining forests of Chile and the Pacific Northwest.

Not only are the two forest regions alike in terms of climate, geography, ecology and scenic beauty, they are globally important centers of forest-based industry and economic activity. Both have been severely exploited over the last century to the point that species, communities and genetic diversity are threatened.

Political forces in both regions are wrestling with new environmental policies that will protect forest ecosystems while allowing for a reasonable level of timber harvest. For now, the old ways of thinking about forests as merely products persist, and their future is still in question. With continued cutting and other real but nebulous worries such as global warming, acid rain and atmospheric ozone depletion exacerbating the present state of native forests in both hemispheres, no one can say what similarities might still be drawn between the forests of Chile and the Pacific Northwest by the end of the next century.

Puerto Montt, Chile. ❀ Kiko Anderson

Orca whales roam both coastal regions. ❀ Ken Wilcox

Forest Ecology:
Nature at Work in Chile's Native Forests

In Chile and the Northwest, there is much to be discovered about the ecology of the forest. We know little about mosses, for example, such as how long it takes them to develop in the canopy of a regenerating forest. We know little about the soil that forms in the canopy with its functioning communities of microbes and arthropods. We know little about all the interactions of the ecological continuum spanning all life forms, from the smallest flowering herb to the largest fur-bearing beast.

We do know that fundamental to the development of these rich and mysterious ecosystems is the climate in which they form. During the southern summer months (December-March), a southwesterly flow brings generally fair weather to Puerto Montt and points to the north. In winter (June-September), fair skies are reliable only to the north of the Bío-Bío River. Warm Pacific and cold Antarctic air masses clash between South America and Antarctica, causing much of southern Chile's more miserable weather.

Stonefly

At these latitudes, the circumference of the Earth is almost entirely occupied by oceans. When the air finds land, where the Andes rise out of the sea, immense volumes of moisture are wrung from the air. The rain is so intense for so many months that only those forest species that can tolerate the deluge and the cool shade that spreads heavily across the landscape can survive. In the extreme south, the Andes have less of an effect on climate. The land is notably drier as elevations decrease and the mountains shrink into the Earth.

Wind may be as important as rain as an ecological factor in the forest. Wind is a principal agent of pollination for some Chilean trees. Several native tree species like araucaria, the cypresses, and all the *nothofagus* and *podocarp* species are very old and their ancestors evolved long before the first insects appeared. To ensure reproductive success, these trees tend to produce huge amounts of pollen grains carried by the wind. The pollen is so thick in araucaria forests that during peak periods it has been referred to as "sulfur rain."

Wind also intensifies freezing and evapotranspiration processes in the forest. As a result, plants grow stunted or deformed, like the "flag trees" of coastal environments or "krummholz" in alpine areas. In both instances, the windward side protects foliage on the leeward side. Coihue and ñirre flag trees are conspicuous in the Magellanic Rainforest. Boldo and olivillo are typical flag trees in central Chilean forests. Lenga and cordilleran cypress often form krummholz, prostrate and deformed along windy ridges.

Wind can also do severe damage within forest ecosystems and human activities can exacerbate the effects. For example, wind velocities can double or triple over a deforested area compared to wind speeds recorded before the trees were cut.[28] The upshot: more serious windfall adjacent to a cutover area than what might have occurred in the same storm if the forest was still intact.

Like wind and rain, fire can be an important factor, although not usually in rainforests. Fires do occur even though lightning storms are uncommon throughout Chile. Through the ages, volcanos are thought to have caused most of the natural forest fires. Nevertheless, the extent and effect of natural fire rarely constitutes a serious threat to a healthy ecosystem. If it did, a forest subjected to frequent massive burns over the millennia probably would not be here today.

Human-caused fires are different, however, and they can be "tremendously destructive" according to Claudio Donoso, a leading forest ecologist in Chile.[29] Huge human-caused fires in the Aisén Province claimed most of the lowland forests long ago, including many of the islands offshore. It is estimated that 1.2 million hectares have been burned by intentionally set fires since the 1940s.[30]

Still, fire has an important role in some native forests in Chile. Several species are known to sprout from burned stumps after a fire, including quillay, ruil, roble, raulí, araucaria and possibly alerce. Some species rely on fire to assist with germination.

In both fire- and landslide-prone areas where mineral soils are exposed, coihue is often a pioneer species. Yet coihue and raulí, among others, have relatively thin bark and are easily damaged. Araucaria bark up to 14 cm thick helps protect the tree from fires that occur in summer and in drier habitats.

The resinous foliage of cordilleran cypress can explode into flames during an intense fire. If fire occurs over thin soils

Otter

or steep slopes, it may destroy the organic material that holds forest soils together. After a fire, soils might easily be washed away by rain. Forest fires also release huge volumes of nitrogen to the atmosphere, although much of it will eventually be recycled by soil microbes back into the forest.

Fire and wind are important to the reproductive cycle of many plants, yet biological factors are just as crucial, if not more so. Almost ninety percent of all trees and shrubs in temperate Chile and Argentina are pollinated through biotic mechanisms.[31] Most trees are insect-pollinated including ulmo, laurel, tepa, lingue, olivillo, canelo, avellano and radal, all of which are mixed with *Nothofagus* in the *siempreverde* and coihue-raulí-tepa forest types.

Other insect-pollinated trees like quillay, boldo and peumo are dominants in the sclerophyllous and mattoral forests of Mediterranean Chile. Many red-flowered plants including Chile's national flower, the *copihue*, are pollinated by hummingbirds.

Mycorrhizal, or root/fungus, associations are extremely important in wet temperate forests. Fungi are much more abundant in moist places with acidic soils, so they are less of a factor in the northern reaches of the forest. In the Chilean rainforests, coihue, ñirre, raulí, roble and lenga all depend on mycorrhizal fungi to help break down compounds containing nitrogen, potassium, calcium and phosphorus into forms that plant roots can absorb. The trees, in turn, contribute carbon and energy to mycorrhizal fungi.

The relationship between trees and fungi is not always symbiotic, however. Some fungi induce heart rot and others are parasitic. And certain *Nothofagus* species are prone to fungal damage, particularly to the roots of older trees.

There are other parasitic plants in the forest, as well. Traum is a large shrub that wraps around ulmo and tineo trees like a constricting vine, eventually killing them. At the same time, there are plants called *epiphytes* that grow on the limbs and trunks of trees, but since they do not obtain water or nutrients from them, they are not parasitic. Lichens and mosses are the most common epiphytes of the far south (just as they are in the Pacific Northwest). There are a few seed-bearing epiphytes in the rainforest as well, like the chupalla or poe plant (*Fascicularia bicolor*), an attractive bromeliad.

Forest predators also fill important niches in the ecosystem. These include insects, birds and mammals. Beetles, flies and butterflies and their larvae nibble on leaves, shoots and cambium. Large green katydids and a wide diversity of creeping, crawling, jumping, flying bugs do their part to sustain the microdynamics of the ecosystem.

Insect damage is generally a phenomenon of non-native forests. For example, introduced Monterey pine plantations in Chile have experienced a number of costly infestations. The polilla del brote (*lepidoptera*) from Argentina has been considered a plague since 1985. A beetle (*Buprestis novemmaculata*) attacks the alien pine in central Chile and in New Zealand, where plantation forestry is more advanced than anywhere else. Eucalyptus plantations have been devoured by *Phoracantha semipunctata*, also from Argentina.

In the late 1970s, two species of native rodents attacked pine plantations by stripping the bark off trees. Up to thirty percent of the trees were killed in some locations. In the 1950s non-native beavers were introduced to Tierra del Fuego for trapping. They spread rapidly and began to strip the trees from lowland riparian areas, stopping up swift-flowing streams. the streams provided habitat for the remarkable torrent duck which depends on turbulent, oxygen-rich water as it swims beneath the surface to feed on stonefly larvae and other delicacies. To date, the beaver has not managed to swim across the Strait of Magellan. If it does, it could pose a major threat to continental ecosystems.

The larger native herbivores like guanaco, huemul and pudu exist as very limited populations and cause no harm to the forest. non-natives like sheep and cows, on the other hand, eat and/or trample herbs, shrubs, young growth and seedlings, causing serious damage, especially in deciduous forests of roble and raulí, among others. Domestic mammals displace wildlife, compact or erode soils amd pollute water. (At least one research ecologist regards the problem so serious worldwide that he has labeled it "bovine imperialism"!)

Rabbit populations have been known to explode in drier, open forests, quickly denuding ground cover. Rats and mice eat seeds and nuts of the avellano and hualo trees, perhaps filling a niche that in North America is occupied by

Tepa

squirrels, a small mammal that never found its way to Chile. Foxes are native nut filchers, preferring avellano, peumo and litre trees.

Some vertebrates, including many bird and mammal species, serve a beneficial role in distributing seeds in the forest. The chucao, Chile's national bird, probably eats (and excretes) most of the seeds that are consumed by animals in the coihue-raulí-tepa forest.[32]

In most cases, the "damage" done by wildlife is not damage at all, but part of the natural equilibrium: the interdependency among species and natural cycles within an ecosystem. Not only are plants well adapted to being nibbled on by insects, birds and mammals, many might not even exist if faunal species were not present. The progeny of some trees, podocarps especially, are assisted by mammals who catch the seeds in their fur or by birds who eat the seeds and then deposit them elsewhere. In some instances, this brief exposure to digestive juices may be required before the seed can germinate.[33]

Birds are an important part of the identity of forested Chile. A unique avian species making good use of Chilean forest ecosystems is the green-backed fire-crown hummingbird, which makes a nest in bamboo using moss and spider webs for raw materials. The bird squats in the nest, slows its metabolism and rests. Rare red-backed hawks and Magellanic woodpeckers are found in araucaria and southern beech forests, and Andean condors sail among the peaks and clouds like golden eagles in the Cascade Mountains of the Pacific Northwest. Chattering choroy parrots congregate in open-canopy forests as swiftly moving flocks of green.

Finally, amphibians and reptiles add their colors to the mosaic of the forest. Unfortunately, we know little about them. We do know that among these two classes of animals Chile has the highest concentration of endemic species of any country in South America.[34] The Darwin frog is one of the more interesting amphibious creatures.

If threatened, it will plop into the water belly up, then float away camouflaged by a variety of markings on its underside.

Strangely, amphibian populations have declined catastrophically around the world in recent years, perhaps a consequence of the widespread destruction of wetlands or increased ultraviolet radiation caused by thinning of the ozone layer—a major concern in southern Chile. Although a number of lizards and other reptiles may also be threatened, only minimal research on their population and distribution in Chilean forests has been conducted.

While the literature is full of details about a multitude of selected organisms in Chile, there is a general consensus among biologists and ecologists that we have only begun to investigate their relationship to the ecology of native forests.

With increased support for research and a comprehensive understanding of creatures and ecosystems, ecologists may be able to help us understand forest ecosystems far better than we do now. They can also help us adopt the constructive attitudes, agreements and policies that are needed if we as a global society are to secure the future of all life in the forest.

Cyttaria fungus grows in globular clusters around a woody burl (called a "llao-llao") in southern beech trees. The yellow fungus associates with lenga in a colorful display against a backdrop of translucent leaves. A similar bright orange cyttaria grows in Magellanic coihue trees, turning milky white as it matures. Southern beech-Cyttaria associations nicely exemplify the interdependency of species within ecosystems. ❀ Peter McBride

Forests of the Far South

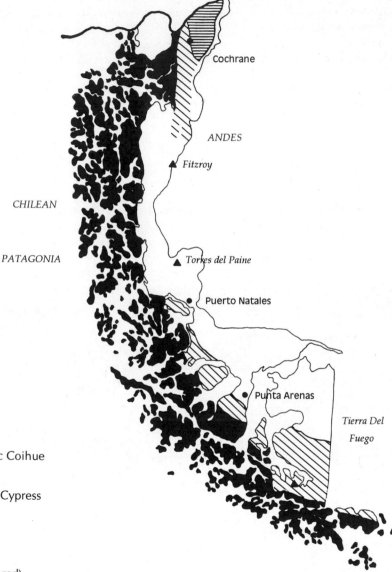

CHILEAN

PATAGONIA

ANDES

▲ Fitzroy

▲ Torres del Paine

● Puerto Natales

Cochrane

● Punta Arenas

Tierra Del Fuego

■ Magellanic Coihue

🌲 Guaitecas Cypress

▨ Lenga

▤ Lenga (altered)

□ Non-Forested

Sources: Ovington, 1983; Donoso, 1983

1.3 The Far South

ONE OF THE WILDEST COASTAL FOREST REGIONS of the world is found in Chilean Patagonia, a great sweeping arc of islands, mountains and fiords that extend for more than 1,000 kilometers south of the Valdivian Rainforest. South of 43° S, the Valdivian Rainforest merges with the North Patagonian Rainforest, a similar bioregion but with a cooler climate, less abundant rainfall and a notable reduction in species diversity. Beyond 48° S, the composition of the coastal rainforest is further diminished to the point that it is recognized separately as the Magellanic Rainforest.[35] These are the planet's southernmost forests, extending all the way to Tierra del Fuego at the tip of the South American continent.

The climate of the far south is uniformly cool and wet year-round, especially in the Magellanic Rainforest, where only a handful of tree species are known to exist. Although trees and many other plants are very slow-growing here, there is no distinct period of dormancy. Oddly enough, some flowering plants bloom all year.

Chile's far south is not all rainforest, however. A long narrow band of outer islands and exposed headlands supports very little forest development. Instead, a pristine coastal moorland of bogs, tussock and bare rock lines much of the Pacific shore. Slightly inland, where soils and other conditions are more tolerable for trees, the rainforest occurs. A third band of vegetation, a deciduous southern beech forest mostly comprised of lenga, is found on the higher slopes and on the undulating lowlands of the extreme south where snowfall may be greater but the rains are not as intense. There are no clear boundaries, of course, between any of these forests.

In the lowland areas of the North Patagonian Rainforest, Chile's three evergreen species of southern beech (the coihues) are often found mixed with tineo, prickly-leaved mañio, canelo and short-leaved mañio. The latter along with common coihue (*N. dombeyi*) and some of the understory plants disappear altogether in the Magellanic Rainforest, where Magellanic coihue becomes the dominant tree.

Magellanic Coihue

(*Nothofagus betuloides*), one of Chile's three evergreen southern beech trees, is the predominant tree of the Magellanic Rainforest. It can be found in lesser numbers in the Valdivian and North Patagonian Rainforests and is well distributed in the Coastal Range, the Andes and southern archipelagos.

The tree is very attractive with a full trunk and layered foliage not unlike the common coihue. The wood is strong and has been used extensively in building construction and furniture-making.

Magellanic Rainforest coast, Tierra del Fuego.
❀ Peter McBride

Ñirre

(Nothofagus antarctica) is a small deciduous southern beech tree that thrives in the cold climate of high-elevation lenga and arau-caria forests in south-central Chile. Farther south, it is much more common at lower elevations in the North Patagonian and Mag-ellanic Rainforests. Ñirre is one of the few tree species that can tolerate the cold, wet and windy climate of Tierra del Fuego. Its prin-cipal use to humans is firewood.

Magellanic coihue grows exceptionally well on some of the worst sites, including places where peat layers are two meters deep. Quila is abundant in the northern portions of the rainforest. Vines and epiphytes, many of them ferns and mosses, are common throughout both rainforest regions. The most widely distributed conifers are the Guaitecas cypress, which is most common in the northern islands, and prickly-leaved mañio, which is scattered along forest borders as far south as Bernardo O'Higgins National Park.

Some experts have suggested that Chile's southern forests may be shifting or receding westward due to a gradual climate warming in the region.[36] The Patagonian steppe on the Argentine side of the Andes appears to be displacing the drier lenga forests at some locations. However, livestock grazing, intentional fires and other human-caused disturbances could explain this apparent shifting of ecotones. Regardless of the cause, there is concern that the extremely slow-growing forests in these regions are very fragile and particularly vulnerable to further disturbances.

In rainforests, newly cleared areas are susceptible to inundation by quila, a dense canopy of bamboo that fills in so rapidly that it seriously impedes forest regeneration. Fuelwood collection, urban and rural settlements and industrial development have also been responsible for a gradual shrinking of Chile's southern forests.

Forest exploitation in the North Patagonian Rainforest and Tierra del Fuego was not a major concern until after 1930, when large-scale clearing and burning of rainforest and lenga forests began in earnest. Perhaps as much as three million hectares have been burned or cleared for sheep and cattle grazing throughout the south.[37] In the northern reaches, island forests were burned aggressively in order to access the valuable rot-resistant timber of the Guaitecas cypress. Much of the Magellanic Rainforest, on the other hand, has remained intact until very recent times. Harsh weather, remoteness and the scarcity of people in the region precluded, or rather delayed, large-scale exploitation of these vast forests.

However, a new trend began to emerge in the 1980s. As far south as Tierra del Fuego, major investments are being made by international firms to acquire large blocks of forest and to construct chipping and lumber processing plants and shipping ports to facilitate the extraction of Patagonia's wealth of wood fiber. Large-scale wood chip exports, mostly to Japan, began in 1991.

International aluminum companies are also planning billion-dollar hydroelectric power, smelter and port developments in the most remote regions to take advantage of low-cost energy and labor.[38] Huge stands of native forest are at risk. Increasing world markets for raw materials, advancing technologies and improved shipping facilities throughout the south have made these delicate forests more vulnerable to destruction than ever before.

Today, large areas of Chile's far south are still as wild and remote as any other place in the Americas. Yet the region is also "filled by a painful emptiness," observed one recent visitor.[39] The native people who occupied this region when the European conquistadors arrived five centuries ago, the Alacalufe, Ona and Yagan, are gone. So are the nomadic Chonos who, for thousands of years, paddled open canoes along the shores of the Valdivian Rainforest to the north. Where the old forest remains intact, we can behold an almost identical scene where many of the same trees that these innocent people witnessed so long ago still stand. No one can begin to predict what these forests will look like in another 500 years.

On the brighter side, large continuous blocks of public land have been protected in the southernmost regions of Chile. In fact, Regions XI and XII account for more than 11 million hectares or 86% of the country's total inventory of protected wildlands. *Isla Magdalena*, a cooperative forest preservation initiative of the Lahuen Foundation, Ancient Forest International and the Chilean government, brightens the picture even more (see "*Isla Magdalena*," Section 3.2). While this bodes well for much of the Magellanic Rainforest, representative ecosystems are not well protected over parts of the North Patagonian Rainforest and the extreme south. And lenga forests comprise only a minor portion

Tineo

(Weinmannia trichosperma) is a large tree found in all of Chile's rainforests, from 35° to 45° S. Tineo grows to 30 meters tall and is often found in marshy areas in the company of ulmo, mañio, tepa and coihue. The dark reddish wood produces attractive, high quality lumber used in general construction and finish work.

Guaitecas Cypress

(Pilgerodendron uviferum)
is a commercially valuable tree that grows near water or in very wet soils in the islands and humid lowlands of southern Chile. Its range extends from Valdivia through Chiloé and the Guaitecas and Chonos Islands, and all the way to Tierra del Fuego.

Trees more than two meters across and 3,000 years of age may have existed only 100 years ago. Although many stands have been destroyed or degraded by fire this century, mature trees up to 40 meters in height and a meter in diameter can still be found. The wood is excellent quality and highly resistant to decay. Guaitecas cypress has been used for posts, piling, boat-building and furniture.

of designated parks and reserves. (The need for protecting these ecosystems is discussed in Part 3.)

Within this mostly mysterious landscape there are three principal forest types: the Magellanic Coihue, Guaitecas Cypress and Lenga Forests. Alerce and *Siempreverde* forests are generally restricted to the Valdivian Rainforest region and are discussed in the previous section.

Coihue de Magallanes Forest

(Magellanic Coihue)

The vast Magellanic Rainforest of the far south is dominated by a single species — and one of Chile's loveliest — the **Magellanic coihue**. This large broadleaf evergreen forms a consistent canopy of green throughout the year, accounting for more than half of all the trees in the southernmost rainforest. As a forest type, it occurs generally south of Aisén from 47° to 56° S at Tierra del Fuego.

The tree is occasionally found in Chile's northern rainforests where it is associated with common coihue, alerce or Guaitecas cypress. Tineo, fuinque, canelo, notro, sauco del diablo and prickly-leaved mañio are more frequent associates in the south. In fall, the Magellanic coihue forest forms a striking contrast with deciduous lenga forests at higher elevations and in the extreme south where some mixing of the two species occurs.

The Magellanic coihue forest occupies a cool wet environment subject to regular winter snowfall in the southern portions and heavy rains throughout. Over seven and a half meters (25 feet) of snow has been recorded in some areas. Understory in the south tends to be relatively sparse compared to the north, where a dense shrub layer of quila and dwarf canelo is more typical.

Little is known about this sprawling, somewhat linear forest, mainly because it is so remote. Weatherwise, the area is less than ideal as a place to carry out intensive fieldwork. Yet, there may be important secrets here, perhaps even new species waiting to be discovered by ambitious researchers. The Magellanic coihue rainforest is wild and intriguing, mostly intact and substantially protected within several of the largest national parks in the world: Laguna San Rafael, Bernardo O'Higgins and Hernando de Magallanes.

Ciprés de las Guaitecas Forest
(Guaitecas Cypress)

Inhabiting stream corridors, coastal areas and relatively flat, poorly-drained areas of southern Chile is a sparse and discontinuous forest type known as the **Guaitecas cypress**. This alerce-like conifer is the dominant tree of the forest. It is found between 40° and 54° S, especially in the Chonos and Guaitecas Island archipelagoes south of Chiloé.

The forest occurs near *siempreverde* and Magellanic coihue forest types. Associated species include Chiloé coihue, prickly-leaved mañio and occasionally tineo and ñirre in the northern part of its range and Magellanic coihue and canelo to the south.

The Guaitecas cypress is frequently surrounded by a tangled understory of tepú *(Tepualia stipularis)*. These *tepuales* are usually so dense that it is almost impossible for woodcutters to access the prized cypress trees. Thus, setting fire to the understory in summer has provided the principal means of exploiting the forest since the early 1900s. As a result, scores of islands in the northern archipelagos have been stripped of their original forest, mostly to obtain poles and posts for agriculture and buildings. One can still find many burned and dead cypress trees in these areas containing wood that is almost perfectly preserved.

Fortunately, the forest may be recovering in many areas. Researchers have noted that where tepú is generally absent, cypress regeneration is quite good. Yet an important ecological relationship between cypress and the tepuales is also assumed. With more careful management of forestry activities in the future, the slow-growing Guaitecas cypress may continue to provide a valuable, albeit limited resource to communities in the region.

Lenga Forest

The deciduous **lenga forest** occupies an extensive region of southern Chile. Beginning high in the Andes at 37° South of the equator, this southern beech forest descends to sea level near Tierra Del Fuego at 56° S. In the north, it forms a narrow band of high forest, broadening substantially in the south where it becomes the principal forest type, covering as much as a half-million hectares in Region XII.

Lenga is the most common timberline species throughout its Andean range. In the extreme south, timberline rarely exceeds 800 meters. To the east, the lenga forest merges with the semi-arid Patagonian steppe. Small stands occur in the coastal mountains including the Nahuelbuta Range, although lenga is generally found mixed with other species here.

Lenga

(Nothofagus pumilio) is an exceptionally wide-ranging deciduous southern beech tree. The dominant tree in the higher elevations of the Andes in central Chile, it is well adapted to harsh winter conditions. In the far south, where temperatures are much colder at low elevations, lenga thrives, reaching 40 meters in height at or near sea level, becoming a dwarfed tree at higher elevations. In either locale, it prefers a drier climate than what is typically found in adjacent rainforests. The wood is prized by carpenters and plywood mills and is now the object of a massive commercial "thinning" (and chipping) project in the far south.

Lenga is most often encountered in pure stands, but mixes with araucaria, coihue, raulí, roble and alerce as well. Quila is a common understory plant in lower mixed stands while dwarf canelo and colihue, a non-branching form of bamboo, appear in the higher elevations. In the rainforest regions, the lenga forest merges with the upper limits of the *siempreverde* and Magellanic coihue forest types. Relatively open forests occur to the south.

On the best sites, trees grow to 40 meters in height and up to a meter in diameter, although much smaller dimensions are more common. At the upper limits of its northern range and at lower elevations in the south, lenga can assume a stunted form due to the short growing season and harsh climate at high elevations. Like the araucaria, lenga does well in volcanic soils and is tolerant of cold snowy winters.

In favorable conditions, lenga is a fast-growing tree that can be grown commercially. The light brown wood lacks visible growth rings and is naturally resistant to decay. It is considered a high-quality wood similar to raulí and is suited to both exterior and interior use, including such items as doors, veneers, furniture, shingles and broomsticks. Now, in the 1990s, lenga has suddenly become a major new source of wood chips as well. This is a serious concern in the extreme south where the trees grow much more slowly and exploitation poses a more severe threat than elsewhere in its range.

Low elevation lenga forest, near Tierra del Fuego
❀ Peter McBride

Part 2

Forest Exploitation

W HEN NATURALIST CHARLES DARWIN passed through Chile a century and a half ago to record his observations of unique plant and animal life, he made frequent comments about the forest and, perhaps more emphatically at times, about the absence of forest. Travelling upriver to Valdivia in the summer of 1835 he wrote of "patches of ground cleared out of the otherwise unbroken forest."[40] With a guide, Darwin headed into the Valdivian Rainforest. Lush and obscuring vegetation made his work difficult: "I managed to see singularly little, either of the geology of the country, or of its inhabitants.... There is not much cleared land near Valdivia," he added plainly.

Near the crest of the coast range, Darwin expressed relief at a break in the canopy that allowed a full view of the central plain below. "The view of these open plains was very refreshing, after being hemmed in and buried in the wilderness of trees. The uniformity of a forest soon becomes very wearisome. This west coast makes me remember with pleasure the free, unbounded plains of Patagonia... yet, with the true spirit of contradiction, I cannot forget how sublime is the silence of the forest."[41]

It was never quite clear to Darwin nor to those who followed why lands in the central plain were often devoid of forest. The

Giant alerce stump in a clearcut at Pata Mai.
✿ Ken Wilcox

These pastoral rolling hills of Chile's central plain were largely forested prior to European settlement in the 1800s.

❀ Kiko Anderson

German botanist Baron von Humboldt noticed a similar phenomenon during his own South American travels three decades earlier.[42] Were these open plains the result of clearing by natives over thousands of years, or was an ecological process of some kind keeping these places naturally unforested?

The agrarian Mapuche people, or "people of the land," kept sizeable areas open for crops and livestock, yet no one can say precisely how much land was cultivated or burned during prehistoric times (artifacts and other evidence, unfortunately, have a way of reverting back to soil over time.) Although most of the central plain seems to have been forested at one time or another, a combination of natural and human causes may offer the best explanation for the missing forest.

In his travels, Darwin also noticed that native forests had been seriously degraded or destroyed in other regions of Chile.[43] From the mid-1500s to the early 1800s, most deforestation occurred as the result of burning or clearing for mines, settlements and farms, even where soils were only marginally productive. However, it was not until 1855, two decades after Charles Darwin and the *H.M.S. Beagle* returned to Europe, that people began to destroy forests on a grand scale. Waves of settlers, some Chilean, many European, moved into the south, reducing ancient southern beech and coniferous forests to smoldering stubble, thousands of hectares at a time.

The destruction was so severe that one Chilean ecologist

writes: "...the colonization and parcelization of the land initiated in that year signified a veritable war against the forest."[44] Fires raged and billowing plumes of smoke shut out the sun for weeks on end. Nineteenth century conservationists pleaded for new forest protection laws to end the destruction. However, business and political leaders of the day often viewed the forest in a different light. The famous promoter of Chile, Vincente Pérez Rosales, and others encouraged the development of Chile's vast frontier and invited the world to come invest in her future prosperity. Many people came: Germans, Swiss, French, Italians. Today, in the lowlands of south-central Chile, visitors travelling overland across hundreds of miles of lovely pastoral landscapes are struck by a European flavor to the architecture, the farms and an almost endless sea of fields and pastures rolling out to the horizon. The vast majority of this land was richly forested prior to European settlement.

2.1 War Against The Forest

THE EARLIEST EXPLOITATION OF CHILE'S native forests may have begun 10,000 years ago in the northern sclerophyllous forests. Tribes in the region are thought to have burned some areas intentionally to open the land to cultivation and to improve hunting of guanaco and other wildlife. Eventually, the stately guanaco were hunted out and replaced by llamas and alpacas originally introduced to the region by the Incas. Intensified grazing by these animals further impacted the forest and prevented much of it from ever recovering.[45]

South of the sclerophyllous forests, indigenous people occupied lowland river valleys where fire was often used for similar purposes. At least a million people, many of them belonging to the Picunche, Mapuche, Pehuenche and Huilliche tribes, are thought to have inhabited a large area between Aconcagua and Chiloé when the Spanish arrived in the sixteenth century.[46] Scarce historical records suggest that pockets of deforested (or non-forested) land were scattered throughout this vast ancient homeland.

Along the southern coasts, native people like the Chonos, Onas, Alacalufes and Yamanas were much less destructive, depending more on the forest and sea for sustenance. Fuel for cooking and heating was their principal use of native wood. In the Andean foothills, native forests were essentially untouched

A New Consciousness

"Man employs his intelligence, which makes him very different from the rest of the animals... all the animals and living beings of the land, except man, are controlled by natural laws... [In] a moment of the Earth's history, he has escaped from the control of natural laws, not only in using natural resources and modifying ecosystems, but also, what is really serious, [he is] destroying them....

He has begun to comprehend that to be able to survive in the universe, he should respect natural laws, he should maintain equilibrium with the environment, and he should, finally, limit his activities...

If this awakening of a new consciousness as an organism that belongs to the ecosystem [occurs]... he should recoup the natural equilibrium and, surely, live in a happier world."

Claudio Donoso,
ECOLOGIA FORESTAL [1990]

Monterey pine seedlings at a CONAF nursery west of Temuco in Araucanía (Region IX), central Chile.
❀ Peter McBride

Deforestation is Real

A 1995 study by Chile's Central Bank found that, if current trends continue, the country's native forests will be reduced by 400,000 to 900,000 hectares within the next ten years, and that essentially all productive native forests between Region VI and Region X could be lost within 20 to 25 years. Native forests diminished by 700,000 hectares in the previous decade. The report sparked strong objections from industry representatives, and applause from the environmental community for its candor.

because of rugged terrain and difficult access. The Pehuenche people reached the remote araucaria forests in the higher elevations, but their reverence for the forest and its rich supply of pine nuts precluded any notion of disturbing it. Farther south, dense rainforests and precipitous slopes deterred settlement in most inland areas, with the exception of Chiloé Island, where the Huilliches cleared lands for grazing and cultivation.

The Spanish era of colonization brought more widespread clearing of forests, especially in the central plain near Santiago. Although indigenous groups maintained a sizeable stronghold south of the Bío-Bío River well into the nineteenth century, Spanish and German colonization in Chiloé and the southern Lakes District advanced northward, carving forests into farmland at a stunning and reckless pace. Today, the evidence of the destruction is found in the attractive rolling fields, hedgerows and fencelines that characterize *el campo*.

There are still great woodlands within central Chile's quilted landscape, but they are not always composed of native trees. Since 1974, single-species tree plantations—fast-growing Monterey pine from California and Mexico and eucalyptus from Australia—have spread rapidly across large areas of central Chile. Prior to the mid-1900s, native species supported virtually all commercial forestry activity in the country. The principal commodity was sawn lumber from roble, raulí, coihue, tepa, laurel, olivillo, lingue, ulmo, tineo, canelo, araucaria and alerce. Railroad ties and mining timbers were also produced in great quantities.

All this has changed now. Today, non-native or *alien* species account for the bulk of all revenues generated by the Chilean forest industry, with most of the total coming from pine.

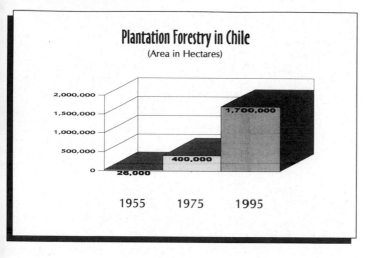

Plantation Forestry in Chile
(Area in Hectares)

Year	Area
1955	26,000
1975	400,000
1995	1,700,000

Pine plantations began to occupy a significant area of land in Chile by the mid-1950s, increasing fifteen-fold within twenty years. In 1974, Decree Law 701 set up a major reforestation program that included substantial government subsidies for planting pine and eucalyptus plantations. As a result of Decree Law 701, plantations rapidly spread across central and south-central Chile, growing to more than 1.7 million hectares by 1995.

Quite by accident, the first Monterey pines were planted in the late 1800s by a gentleman from Concepción who had apparently ordered Douglas fir (better known in Chile as "Oregon pine") seedlings for a small woodlot. He received Monterey pine from California by mistake. As fate would have it, the tree grew three times faster in Concepción than in California. Nevertheless, there was no market at the time for wood chips or pulp, and the quality of pine lumber was inferior to all the native hardwoods. The tree was not particularly good for firewood either. Eucalyptus imported from Australia, also in the late 1800s, burned far better than pine.

Markets for pine pulp and lumber would eventually develop, however. In the 1960s, the industry began to move away from native species as the first small plantations matured in Region VIII, close to Concepción and the Bío-Bío River. By 1990, a full 80 percent of the forest industry was oriented to plantations. Nearly 100,000 additional hectares were planted in 1990. Plantations, or "artificial forests" as some Chileans refer to them, covered 1.7 million hectares (about four million acres) by 1995.[47]

Some plantations occupy degraded lands that became unsuitable for cultivation due to careless logging and agricultural practices. Although the best soils have long since eroded away, these artificial forests manage to thrive, and by industry accounts, actually enhance the quality of eroded soils.[48] A 1987 study conducted by CODEFF, on the other hand, found that artificial forests generate significant long-term soil impacts, including increasing acidity.

In the 1990s, plantation forestry has proved to be such a lucrative enterprise that some of the largest lumber, pulp and paper corporations and financiers in the world are making

Value of native species wood chips exported from Chile:

1987	$0
1990	$56,000,000
1994	$98,500,000

INFOR, 1995

record-breaking investments in land, trees, harvest technologies and equipment, roads, chipping plants, pulp mills, sawmills, and shipping ports in all of Chile's forested and once-forested regions.

As the industry grows, plantations are expanding from the more heavily exploited and developed lowlands into the high-quality native forests of the Andean foothills as well as the coastal mountains to the west. Areas that were not seriously degraded in the past, even the most pristine areas — the last great stands of Chile's original native forest biodiversity and richest remaining unprotected ecosystems — are now threatened.

In the 1990s, CODEFF estimates that 120,000 to 200,000 hectares of native forest are seriously damaged or destroyed each year (CONAF reported a much lower rate in 1995 of 40,000 to 45,000 hectares yearly). Much of the loss is due to clearcut logging and the substitution of pine and eucalyptus plantations, plus high-grading for wood chip production. Industry is not the only culprit in forest destruction, however. Huge losses have occurred from subsistence tree-felling and human-caused forest fires in every forested region of the country. Native forests have been cleared and burned on a massive scale for agriculture and have been heavily cut over for firewood.

The friendly, hard-working people in the countryside, the *campesinos*, those who clear the woods for grazing animals or crops and who gather wood to sell or to provide for their simplest needs — heating, cooking and shelter — account for a significant portion of the deforestation occurring in Chile today.

In 1988, Chile's *Instituto Forestal*, or INFOR, a principal source of statistics for both government and industry analysts, estimated that as much as three-fourths of the total volume of <u>native</u> wood consumed in 1987 was for fuelwood. Urban and rural populations combined consume about seven million cubic meters of native fuelwood yearly.[49] The figures are staggering yet debatable and even misleading, according to environmentalists.

In 1993, CODEFF and the World Wildlife Fund completed a study which found that forest clearing by *campesinos* was far less destructive than harvest activities of the timber and chip industries.[50] A discouraging trend is rapidly emerging in industrial forestry. In the past few years, commercial timber harvest and the conversion of natural forests to pine and eucalyptus plantations have assumed major roles in the destruction of Chile's natural forests, contributing to a total loss of native forests on the order of 700,000 hectares in the last ten years. Chile's Central Bank projected in 1995 that without proper management and protection native forests could essentially be exhausted within 20 to 25 years.

With the return to democracy in 1990 and a more stable political and economic outlook, foreign investments in the

"We don't agree with the replacement of native forests, even degraded forests or old trees... The companies say a lot of forests in Chile are [degraded] and those forests have to be replaced. We don't accept replacement. Degraded forests should be replanted with native species"

Hernán Verscheure,
CODEFF, Santiago

forestry sector are up dramatically. Those who supply expanding world markets for lumber, wood chips, pulp and unprocessed logs have all turned their attention to Chile. Japan, the world's largest forest products purchaser, is leading the way with projected short-term capital investments ranging in the hundreds of millions of dollars.[51]

Still, as bleak as the future of native forests might appear, as much as 80 percent of all revenues earned from forest product exports come from plantations (mostly Monterey pine), not from native forests. Massive tree-planting programs initiated in 1974 in response to government subsidized incentives are beginning to pay substantial dividends as the first big stands of maturing timber are harvested. Native timber, as a result, is not as critical to the nation's forest economy — at least for the time being.

Yet political and economic pressures are on the rise, with influential leaders in government and industry insisting that Chile step up the cutting in native forests, and convert hundreds of thousands of additional hectares to plantations. Others, including former President Patricio Aylwin and his Agricultural Minister have said they are equally concerned about the cultural and ecological impacts that result from more aggressive timber harvesting. The Aylwin government worked to develop national environmental policies and sustainable forest management programs that can support a potent forest industry without destroying native forests — Chile's great symbol of "national patrimony." The new government of Eduardo Frei has expressed similar concerns, but has been criticized for moving too slowly.

While there is evidence that some government leaders are sincere in their efforts, not everyone is convinced. The strongest sentiment expressed by Chileans contacted during the research phase of this report was one of serious apprehension — a general feeling that the government is telling its citizens it wants to protect native forests, while continuing to allow excessive cutting, conversions, and poor management and enforcement. The fear is that in the name of Chilean prosperity the government will back down on real protection for these forests. New legislation that can help establish a clear policy on the future of native forests was introduced in Congress in April, 1992 and has been debated for more than three years. Some critics argue that the legislation goes too far, while others say it does not go far enough. Some version of the law may pass in 1996, but no one expects the controversy to end any time soon.

In some respects, Chile's is a classic situation: a developing nation immensely dependent on its natural resource wealth to stimulate trade and development, to generate income, and ultimately to improve the living standard for its citizens. But like all nations of the world, development and resource exploitation

Forest Uncertainties

Chilean policy makers are on the verge of deciding the fate of their own forests. At the time this work was published, uncertainty remained over how much forest might be protected as parks and reserves, how much might be restored or managed commercially, and how much might be lost to plantations or development.

Following the lead of environmental groups in Chile, Ancient Forest International will be helping to ensure that significant areas are adequately protected in all forest regions, to support the ongoing development of sustainable forestry projects, and where "managed" forests are concerned, to help advance the notion that long-term ecological values should always take precedence over short-term economic gain.

in Chile bring social and environmental costs or impacts that are not always easy to discern. In many countries—and Chile is no exception—exploiting and developing the landscape poses serious implications for native cultures as well. To what extent native people will benefit from or suffer the consequences of new forest policies remains to be seen.

2.2 Los Campesinos

THE LOVELY CHILEAN COUNTRYSIDE, or *campo*, can be a difficult place to make a living. Unless you own a productive farm, a forest or a fishing boat, you may find yourself among the thousands of *campesinos* who migrate into the cities each year seeking employment and a better life. Unfortunately, the cities are so saturated with capable workers that many must settle for the lowest-paying jobs in the service sector, or struggle to survive in shantytowns or "rings of misery" that nearly encircle Santiago and several other large cities.[52] At least eighty percent of Chile's 13.2 million people now make their home in urban areas. The numbers continue to grow, a trend that is more or less typical throughout Latin America.

Despite the exodus to the cities, rural populations have remained relatively stable in recent decades, since population gain has been roughly equivalent to the rate of urban migration. For those who stay behind, it may be just as well to be poor in the *campo* as to be poor in the city. To survive in the *campo*, rural dwellers often depend on the land for all their basic needs. They clear some land for cultivation, more for livestock and to acquire building materials, and still more for firewood.

At present, land cultivation alone is not causing significant deforestation in Chile. The principal reason for this is that productive agricultural soils underlying forest lands are no longer easy to find. The most fertile areas were claimed and cleared long ago. In many instances, the best agricultural lands are under large commercial ownerships that can be traced to the days of Spanish land grants, a lopsided land distribution system that, to this day, has left most of the land in the hands of a few, in spite of major land reforms in the 1960s and 1970s. Most land that is available and affordable, regardless of whether or not it is presently forested, is likely to be better suited to livestock than to growing crops. Thus, where *campesinos* are concerned, animals usually have the run of the land.

"...the haves of the world are still treating the have-nots as the colonies of old were treated, and this has a bad effect upon what irreplaceable wilderness we have left... the haves are destroying wilderness by ricochet."
—David Brower
LET THE MOUNTAINS TALK,
LET THE RIVERS RUN [1995]

El campo, a rural homestead in the southern Lakes Region. The land was once buried in rainforest.
❀ Ken Wilcox

In order to eke out a living, a family farmer must produce a supply of meat, wool and other products, a portion of which must be sold or traded to obtain whatever goods cannot be produced on the farm. But if too many cows, pigs or sheep are crowded into a given area to graze, forage is quickly depleted, soils are compacted, drainage and erosion problems develop, and the land loses its already limited productivity. In the search for more pasture, the *campesino* looks to adjacent wooded areas. More forest is burned or otherwise opened up, and the process of soil and forest degradation is repeated. The collection of firewood for heating and cooking, of course, only exacerbates the situation, especially in the cooler regions to the south where the need for heating is greater.

Both original and second-growth forests are easily damaged, even where they are not entirely cleared. Animals feed on grasses, herbs, shrubs and trees, including young plants, roots, seedlings, saplings and new growth close to the forest floor. If over-grazed, beneficial plant communities may be destroyed, forcing the animals and their keepers to seek out new ground. At the same time, the finest trees are often harvested for firewood or for sale to local sawmills, leaving behind what is commonly referred to as a *degraded* forest, a scraggly mess of diseased and distorted trees. Some experts have expressed concern that such practices impact not only the natural equilibrium, species composition and overall health of a forest, but also the genetic stock from which future forests might emerge.[53]

On a much smaller scale, *campesinos* also harvest several native species for uses other than firewood. Quillay bark and leaves are collected—often poached—for *saponin*, a cleaning agent also used in fire extinguishers and insecticides. Unfortunately, bark stripping can be deadly for the quillay, and strict requirements have been adopted to protect the tree. Leaves of the boldo tree are picked and dried for making a popular Chilean tea. The leaves contain *boldine*, a medicinal derivative used in treating liver ailments and digestive problems. Both products have been exported in significant quantities for many years, generating close to $1 million in export revenues in 1990.[54]

Finally, an emerging issue that involves the felling of native trees by *campesinos* concerns the growing markets for pulpwood and wood chips. No hard data is available, but there are indications that the price some chipping plants pay for raw native logs is now competitive with the value of the same logs sold for firewood. Any difference in price might be offset by the fact that the seller does not have to chop the wood for the customer.

In 1989, a *vara* of firewood piled in the forest sold for about US$1 (*vara* is the popular measurement for firewood and amounts to about 1/4 of a cubic meter of wood). A "standard" pile of logs at a logging site, called a *metro-ruma*, contains 2.4 cubic meters of wood or about 10 times the wood volume in a *vara*. One *metro-ruma* was selling for US$10, or 10 times the price of a *vara*, thus a forest worker with an axe and a chain saw could earn about US$4 for each meter of wood cut. In the same year, a similar volume of firewood in the Pacific Northwest sold for about $15-20. Since 1989, the rising value of a *metro-ruma* has been closely related to the increasing demands of the chipping industry.

As discussed in the next section, the wood chip industry has literally exploded into existence since 1987, and by all indications will continue to grow dramatically for some time. Lumbering, which employs *campesinos* as well as urban dwellers, is also on the rise, although native forest-dependent sawmills represent only a small fraction of the pine-dominated forest products industry. However, wood chip and pulp industries pose startling consequences for native forests and the fuelwood supply.

Native Fuelwood Consumption (1990)
(Cubic meters / %)

Urban heating & cooking	3,486,056	47.5
Rural heating & cooking	3,470,711	47.3
Industrial uses	171,109	2.3
Service sector	143,236	2.0
Commercial baking	65,936	0.9
Total	7,337,048	100.0

Source: P. Donoso, 1991

Fuelwood Consumption

Campesinos certainly cut a lot of native wood, but urban and rural populations nationwide may each be responsible for more than 47 percent of the seven million cubic meters of native-species fuelwood consumed each year.[55] The balance, about 5 percent, is used for commercial and industrial purposes.

The heaviest consumers of native fuelwood are in the south, where the climate is colder and wetter than in the rest of Chile. In northern and central Chile, consumption is reduced by warmer, drier weather and the availability of plantation timber and wood waste from sawmills.

Even though the demand for firewood in the arid north is not great, minimal tree growth means far less wood is available per person, perhaps less than 1/100th of a cubic meter per year in some areas.[56] In the heavily populated regions of central Chile, where there is reduced forest cover and low to moderate forest productivity, nature is providing no more than 0.8 cubic meter of native wood per person per year. Here, eucalyptus provides an important supplement to the wood supply. In the more productive forests of southern Chile, at least 2.5 cubic meters are available per person each year.

Annual per capita fuelwood consumption in Chile is approximately 1.2 cubic meters, compared to 1.03 cubic meters for all of Latin America (people in Africa and Asia generally consume more than twice that amount). In the south, the demand is much higher, probably around two cubic meters — still less than what is theoretically available.

Although something on the order of 15 million cubic meters of fuelwood are burned nationwide each year, as much as half the total is from non-native species, essentially eucalyptus and pine. About 7.3 million cubic meters are derived from native species. This represents more than a third of the 20 million cubic meters of new wood thought to be produced in Chile's native forests each year.[57]

Non-Native Trees & the Demand for Fuelwood

The most productive native forests in the country are found in Region X, where 80 percent of all native wood cut was used for fuelwood (prior to the emergence of the chipping industry). Here in the rainforest region, and in the far south, exotic species are much less prevalent, so native species make up almost the entire wood supply. In the northern regions, native trees like *espino* (acacia) and *litre* provide much of the fuelwood, although CONAF has been experimenting recently with eucalyptus plantations in an effort to relieve the pressure on scarce supplies of native wood. While pine is a poor-quality wood for burning, eucalyptus is recognized as one of the best. It grows exceptionally well in a variety of environments and may prove invaluable in the development of environmentally sound fuelwood production strategies throughout much of the country.

*Mill-bound native
forest timber.*
❀ Alex Clapp

Annual Forest Exports
(\$US Millions)

1982	332.1
1983	326.2
1984	382.7
1985	334.6
1986	403.1
1987	577.3
1988	730.3
1989	783.6
1990	855.3
1991	1,050.0
1992	1,125.8
1993	1,207.1
1994	1,564.3
1995	~2,300.0

[Figures not adjusted for inflation.]
Source: INFOR, 1995

2.3 The Forest Industry Boom

THE FOREST PRODUCTS INDUSTRY IN CHILE is growing at a record pace. The total value of lumber, fiberboard, wood chip and pulp exports in 1995 was at an all-time high, with all forest exports combined surpassing $2.3 billion.[58] This represents a 100 percent increase over 1992 and is triple the 1989 level. Growth in the industry in the 1980s occurred at twice the rate of the nation's economy as a whole, led by pulp, paper and wood chips. Over half of 1995 forest exports involved wood pulp or cellulose.

Export figures for 1993 ($1.2 billion) suggested less vigorous growth due to a dramatic 40 percent drop in world wood pulp prices. However, 1994 exports of $1.6 billion were again at record highs with improved world markets. Growth in 1995 was simply astounding. With new cellulose and wood chipping plants and large volumes of Monterey pine rapidly becoming available, the industry is likely to continue its skyward surge in coming years. Exports have already exceeded the $1.8 billion figure projected by CONAF for the year 2000. CONAF anticipated that yearly forest exports would exceed $2.9 billion by the year 2010. Those numbers now appear to be much too conservative. In any event, forest export values in 1995 were second only to Chilean copper.

These remarkable trends can be attributed to two major factors. First, vast areas of Monterey pine established in the 1970s are now mature enough to be harvested profitably. Pine is a major new export commodity in Chile not previously available for such large-scale exploitation.

Secondly, forest exports and world demand for wood and paper products climbed steadily after 1985 in response to the general rebound in the world economy that followed the early-1980s recession. Furthermore, the early 1990s slowdown in the industrialized world seems not to have interrupted Chile's vibrant economy, nor the world's huge appetite for wood and paper. The government projects sustained 5 to 7 percent annual growth nationwide, low inflation (under 12%) and unemployment under 5 percent. The number of people living in extreme poverty is also on the decline.

Why the boom in the forest industry? More people in the

Rio Condor

In remote Tierra del Fuego, a Washington State company with a history of clearcut logging methods is moving ahead with a $200 million investment scheme that will turn much of a 10,000-year-old lenga rainforest near Rio Condor into furniture lumber and wood chips.[59] Touted as a "sustainable forestry" project, 70 percent of the trees in targeted blocks of forest may be cut, while some areas would be left unlogged as park or natural reserve.

About 250,000 hectares were purchased by the Trillium Corporation (known as *Forestal Trillium Ltda*. in Chile) in 1993—on the heels of a complaint by CODEFF that five companies already controlled more than 160,000 hectares of native forest elsewhere in the country. Opposition is building in Chile to the concentrated ownership of large parcels of native forest by just a few corporations.

[Continued on p. 58...]

world are demanding more wood fiber (pulp, paper, chips and lumber. With today's renewed democracy in Chile, healthy economic forecasts and ever-expanding world markets for wood fiber, major Japanese, U.S., Canadian and New Zealand corporations, among others, are rushing to meet the demand. All are making enormous investments in forest land, chipping plants, sawmills, pulp and paper mills, and port facilities.

Japan's Ambassador to Chile projected in 1991 that Japanese corporate investments alone in Chilean forestry were likely to increase from $35 million in 1990 to as much as $600 million within six years—nearly a twenty-fold increase.[60] Mitsubishi, Daio Paper and Marubeni are among the major players. Japan and Western Europe, principally Belgium and West Germany, are the foremost purchasers of Chilean wood and pulp.

Major new cellulose plants involving investments from $500 million to more than $1 billion were completed in 1991 and 1992. Developments include at least three new pulp mills, the largest being a $500 million bleached-pulp mill on the Bío-Bío River by a Scott Paper, Shell and Citibank consortium. Another $1 billion pulp mill was proposed in 1995 for Valdivia.

Investments may be slowing, however, with so much production capacity already on line. A billion-dollar cellulose plant proposed in Region X was put on hold early in 1993 due to a surprise drop in the world market for pulp. Prices were down from $760/ton in 1989 to $300-400/ton in 1993, then rose again to $850/ton in 1995. A slight decrease was expected in 1996. Major investments are planned to handle the movement of raw and processed materials, including the development of two new wood chip shipping ports, west of Puerto Montt and at Valparaíso. Investors have also purchased large blocks of forest land, sometimes disrupting area residents.

Several large chipping plants are under construction in southern Chile, and another was recently completed in Pucón, to the ire of local officials and business owners who depend on healthy forests for tourism. Despite the huge supply of pine chips flowing through international markets, 60 percent of the chips exported from Chile in 1994 were from native species. Sawmills are expanding, as are facilities for producing particle board, wafer board and paneling. In 1996, one of the largest lumber and chipping operations in Chile will begin in the lenga forests of Chile's far south—the southernmost forests on the planet.

From Tierra del Fuego to the heart of Siberia, no virgin forest in the world is far enough removed from industrialized society for its future to be secure. As we slip toward a new milennium, we are consuming resources and destroying nature at an ever-increasing rate. And we have yet to appreciate the consequences of these actions beyond our own lifetimes.

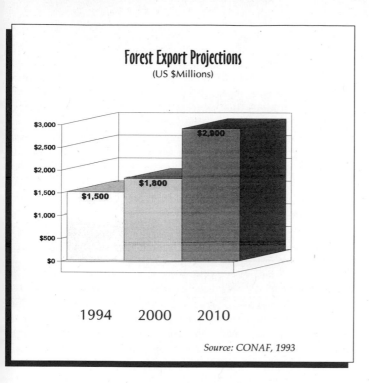

Forest Export Projections
(US $Millions)

$3,000
$2,500
$2,000
$1,500 — $1,500
$1,000
$500
$0

$1,800

$2,000

1994   2000   2010

Source: CONAF, 1993

Plantations (1994)

Species	Hectares	Acres	Percent
Monterey pine	1,375,886	3,398,438	78.7
Eucalyptus	238,312	588,631	13.6
Atriplex	47,232	116,663	2.7
Tamarugo	20,622	50,936	1.2
Douglas fir	12,379	30,576	0.7
Alamo	3,798	9,381	0.2
Algarrobo	3,238	7,998	0.2
Others	46,056	113,758	2.7
Totals	**1,747,523**	**4,316,381**	**100.0**

Source: INFOR, 1995

Conversion of Native Forests to Plantations

Rio Condor

[Continued from p. 56...]
To their credit, Trillium officials promise to adhere to the precepts of sustainability, and Chilean scientists have been hired to study the area's ecology and assist in developing a forest plan. Major concerns include the outright loss of primary forest, potential wind damage, habitat disruption, impacts to thin soils, and problems with forest regeneration in this marginally productive ecosystem.

Despite the low cost of forest land and standing timber in Chile's far south, the industry at large continues to resist small-scale sustainable harvest methods that do not destroy the forest in the process. At the same time, Trillium's apparent commitment to an ecosystem-based approach to logging is commendable and should be encouraged throughout the forest industry in Chile, if not the world.

One of the most contentious forest projects ever proposed in Chile was "Forestal Corral," a proposal by Terranova S.A. and the Japanese giant Marubeni to convert up to 23,000 hectares of native forest to eucalyptus plantations in the coastal mountains near the city of Valdivia.[61] An additional 12,400 hectares was to be "managed" for chips and reforested with native species. Perhaps 90 percent of the area targeted had never been logged. What was most unsettling about the project is that the area of native forest in question may be one of the most biologically diverse ecosystems in the country.

The Terranova project and the upswing in forest exploitation generally have not gone unnoticed by Chilean environmentalists. They strongly opposed Forestal Corral for several reasons. The region is blanketed by a classic *siempreverde* forest comprising an important part of the largest remaining area of undisturbed Valdivian Rainforest. Terranova is also within an area of Chile most lacking in protected wildlands. This coastal region south of Valdivia is so wild that scientists are uncertain about the true diversity of plant and animal species that exist there.

One major concern was that logging and road development would open adjoining areas to exploitation, setting an undesirable precedent for similar projects in the future. Terranova would double the amount of chips coming from native forests in Chile. If approved, perhaps no forest in the nation would be secure from the looming threat posed by the multinational chipping industry. The project was withdrawn in early 1993 in response to new forest legislation prepared by the government. In its wake environmentalists are now battling an even larger scheme designed to replace up to 180,000 hectares of "brush" (young or degraded forest) with pine and eucalyptus.

Chilean and international environmental groups appealed to the President, to CONAF and to the public to establish new protected areas, to develop meaningful native forest management policies, and to work toward restoring — not replacing — degraded portions of the country's original native forests. Acting in part on these concerns, the Aylwin administration appointed at least two special commissions to develop recommendations involving a variety of native forest issues and related environmental problems. Existing policies were found to be inadequate if Chile is to cope favorably with the growing urgency for sensible, long-term management of limited natural resources.

Mount "Puerto Montt:" For some, huge stockpiles of wood chips are a kind of economic indicator. For others, they are a source of dismay: fermenting gases, foul odors, noise and water pollution. Unsightly mountains of chips like these offer a stark image of the potential fate of Chile's native forests.
❀ Kiko Anderson

Unquestionably, forests are among Chile's most valuable resources and a major component of foreign exchange. Although copper production in the north represents by far the greatest source of national income, forest products from the central and southern regions now account for more than ten percent of the value of all exports—equivalent to all fishing and agricultural exports combined. Thus, productive forests are pivotal to the overall health of the Chilean economy.

Plantation timber is currently satisfying the bulk of the demand. Over a million and a half hectares of pine and eucalyptus have been planted in Chile and another 60 to 90 thousand hectares are being added each year. The momentum of the industry has drawn people from the countryside into the nationwide conversion of native forests to exotic plantations. Plantation "kits" of a thousand seedlings with planting instructions are sold to anyone who wants them. As the best native trees are cut and hauled to chipping plants, the kits effectively speed up the conversion process on small holdings. The cumulative effect, particularly in Region X, could be disastrous if not carefully administered.

No one can deny that growing Monterey pine has proved to be an amazingly successful economic strategy for the forest industry. But the success of these exotic tree farms has, to some extent, come at the expense of native forest ecosystems. Substitution of native forests by alien species is simply unacceptable to many Chileans, according to pollsters. Monocultural forestry contributes to impoverished soils, insect infestation and diminished genetic variability. Where native stands are converted to pine and eucalyptus, impacts are obvious and immediate. What long-term consequences of plantation

forestry might spill over into adjacent native forest ecosystems is unknown.

CONAF generally agrees that plantations need to be carefully regulated to prevent degradation of soils and other adverse impacts. They also agree that new protected areas need to be established in many parts of the country. An alternative approach to managing forest lands that has not been examined at length involves the notion of *sustainable forestry*. Instead of being converted to plantations, some native forests in Chile may be well suited to commercial production using this ecosystem-based management approach to harvesting trees. Sustainable forestry (discussed later in this report) is not something the industry seems eager to invest in, however, at least in ecological terms. Although the corporate rhetoric may sound favorable at times, any real commitment to protecting ecosystems over the long term is often lacking. Selective cuts and rotations in primary forests may be labeled "sustainable" by industrialists, but invariably such practices destroy ecosystems. Ecologically sustainable forestry requires a much softer touch that keeps the forest intact.

Despite the fact that a number of Chilean trees are widely recognized for their high-quality wood, rapid growth, and potentially cost-effective management, the success of Monterey pine and eucalyptus seems to have blinded most investors to the commercial potential of native species. The principal reason for this is simply the rapid rate at which pine matures into marketable wood fiber — 20 to 30 years, compared with 40 to 50 years for the best-growing native species. While the industry at large has essentially overlooked the quality of the resource that native species provide, Chilean forest ecologists have not — but their objectives are not so simple as to substitute a single native species for a single alien species in a tree farm.

Rather, many forest scientists and ecologists would prefer to see some native forests managed for commercial production in ways that are not detrimental to the environment. Using a variety of economic tactics such as reforestation subsidies and the development of specialized international markets, many hope to demonstrate the commercial viability of protecting and restoring some of the remaining stands of Chile's native forests. Convincing the industry will not be an easy task.

Salvage logging in a burned-over forest.
❀ Eric Nill

Commercially Valuable Native Trees

Of Chile's 125 native tree species, about 30 are considered by CONAF and the forest industry to be commercially valuable. Nearly all of these are found south of 35° S. Most abundant are lenga, coihue, olivillo and canelo. Other important species that are readily available include roble, ulmo, tepa, boldo, and two mañio species. Much less common are raulí, Guaiteca cypress, laurel, quillay, hualo, Chilean palm, Magellanic coihue, and coihue of Chiloé. Boldo, quillay, palm and araucaria provide products that do not require felling trees.

Several species are commercially extinct: ruil, tineo, cordilleran cypress, lingue, roble (pellín), laurel, lleuque and two protected species, alerce and araucaria. The first seven could be reestablished through appropriate recovery programs. The last two, alerce and araucaria, have a long history of commercial exploitation and both have been severely depleted. Although dead alerce and araucaria can still be harvested in Chile, live trees are protected. Both are very slow-growing trees that will not be contributing wood fiber to the forest economy any time soon.

Potentially Productive Native Forests*
(By Region, 1994)

Regions	Hectares	Acres	Percent
I - V	6,700	16,600	0.1
VI	41,200	101,800	0.5
VII	196,400	485,100	2.6
VIII	401,700	992,200	5.4
IX	509,600	1,258,700	6.8
X	3,592,600	8,873,700	48.0
XI	1,686,000	4,164,400	22.5
XII	1,059,000	2,615,700	14.1
Total**	**7,493,200**	**18,508,200**	**100.0**

* *"Potentially productive" native forest is defined by INFOR as those lands that contain 30 or more cubic meters of wood per hectare, based on trees over 25 cm in diameter. These lands may or may not be economical to access.*

** *7.5 million hectares represents about 891 million cubic meters of wood.*

Source: INFOR, 1995

Productive Native Forest & Plantations
(By Region, 1994)

Region	Productive Native Forest Hectares	Productive Native Forest Cubic Meters	Plantations Hectares Pine	Plantations Hectares Eucalyptus
I	4,000	100,000	—	162
II-IV	0	—	—	2,684
V	0	—	23,462	38,629
R.M.	2,700	100,000	989	8,618
VI	41,200	1,200,000	73,105	19,670
VII	196,400	6,400,000	314,938	18,058
VIII	401,700	24,100,000	633,672	84,925
IX	509,600	32,100,000	216,408	30,359
X	3,592,600	744,200,000	113,312	35,205
XI	1,686,000	50,600,000	—	2
XII	1,059,000	31,800,000	—	—
Totals	**7,493,200**	**890,600,000**	**1,375,886**	**238,312**

Source: INFOR, 1995

Chilean Export Revenues
By Economic Sector
($US millions/*percent*)

	1970		1980*		1994	
Mining	$950.4	86	$2,771.9	59	$5,107.1	44
Agric./fishing	60.2	5	338.3	7	1,154.4	10
Industry	57.6	5	980.2	21	3,863.6	33
Forestry	43.5	4	580.3	12	1,520.0	13
Total	**$1,111.7**	*100*	**$4,670.7**	*100*	**$11,645.1**	*100*

* *Note: 1980 was an exceptionally good year for forest exports. Revenues dropped
to $323 million in 1983 (or 8% of all exports) then rose sharply again in the late 1980s.*

Source: INFOR, 1995

Chilean Forestry Exports
By Product
($US millions/*percent*)

	1970		1980*		1994	
Chemical pulp	$16.4	39	$197.1	42	$717.7	46
Wood chips	—	0	—	0	163.5	11
Lumber	8.6	21	148.9	32	190.0	12
Newspaper	9.6	23	31.0	7	77.2	5
Raw logs	—	0	56.9	12	113.9	7
Other products	7.1	17	34.2	7	302.0	19
Total	**$41.7**	*100*	**$468.1**	*100*	**$1,564.3**	*100*

* *Note: Chemical pulp, lumber and raw log exports were strong in 1980.
Wood chip exports did not begin until the late 1980s.*

Source: INFOR, 1995

Principal Forest Export Companies
(1990s)

Companies exporting chips from native species:
Aserraderos Unidos (Chile Ltda.)*
Compañia Chilena de Astillas S.A.*
Forestal del Sur Ltda.*
Forestal y Ganadera Monte Alto Ltda.

Astillas Exportaciones Ltd.*
Consorcio Maderero Ltda.*
Forestal Coronel S.A.*
Sociedad Industrial y Comercial Fabril Maderera de la Patagonia Ltda.

* *Also sell wood chips from exotic species.*

Companies selling native pulp logs:
Consorcio Maderero de Magallanes Ltda.　　Forestal del Sur Ltda.

Companies selling native sawlogs:
Compañia Forestal y Maderera Panguipulli S.A.　Complejo Agro-Forestal Chuhuío Ltda.
Forestal del Sur Ltda.

Largest exporting companies (over $10 million):
Andinos S.A.
Aserradero San Vicente S.A.
Aserraderos Unidos (Chile Ltda.)
Celulosa Arauco y Constitucion S.A.*
Celulosa del Pacifico*
Consorcio Maderero Ltda.
Forestal Carampangue S.A.
Forestal e Industrial Santa Fe*
Maderas Nacimiento S.A.

Aserradero Mininco S.A.
Aserraderos Copihue S.A.
Astillas Exportaciones Ltd.
CMPC International Ltda.*
Compañia Chilena de Astillas S.A.
Forestal Arauco S.A.
Forestal del Sur Ltda.
Industrias Forestales S.A.
Papeles Bío-Bío S.A.

* *Principal exporters (CMPC = Compañia Manufacturera de Papeles y Cartones).*
  (Forestal Trillium Ltda. is expected to become a major exporter of lenga chips and lumber in 1996.)

Source: Chilean Forest Export Guide, 1991/CONAF, 1991, CHIP.

2.4 Chilean Forest Management

Forest PROTECTION AND MANAGEMENT IN CHILE can be traced to the 16th century, when the laws and decrees of Spain determined the fate of forests, minerals and other natural wealth in its distant colony on the Pacific. Chilean law began to protect forests and even certain tree species not long after Independence in the early 1800s. The *Novísima Recopilación* proclaimed that "forests shall be conserved, authorizing felling solely of large trees and leaving the plant in such a state that it can regenerate...."[62] Many forests were administered as community property by town councils. Young growing trees were not to be cut, and areas that had been deforested were required to be replanted.

In 1855, land use regulations required citizens to "conserve the forest in its essence." Then, in 1859, the first supreme decree was handed down to control the destruction of alerce in Llanquihue and Chiloé provinces.[63] Regrettably, the lowland alerce forest would be completely annihilated a generation later (see Part 1). The President was given the responsibility of overseeing forest exploitation in 1871, and the first set of forest regulations was adopted twelve years later. New forest laws were established in 1925 and 1931 — some of which are still in force today. Fires were generally outlawed in the 1960s by the Frei government.

The most significant new forest law since 1931 is Decree Law 701, adopted in 1974 by the Pinochet military regime. The law included strong provisions for reforestation and established a framework for the development of Chile's vast pine plantations. Public funds were made available to subsidize up to 75 percent of the cost of planting trees. The law was amended in 1979 to include additional tax incentives for growing trees. From 1980 to 1989, an average of 79,000 hectares was planted annually. Paper manufacturers lobbied for the program, so it is no surprise that so much pulp and paper development is underway now in the 1990s. No doubt, they were enticed by the prospects for cheap electric power, chemicals, land and labor. The program has been a major economic success. Pine pulp has been the most valuable wood product exported since 1982, accounting for more than 40

Deforestation in Chile

The UN's Food and Agriculture Organization (FAO) announced in 1995 that Chile is now the second most deforested nation in the world. FAO expressed concern that Chile also lacks effective legislation to protect its native forests.

Forest Lands in Chile

	Hectares	Acres
Total area of Chile:	75,800,000	187,200,000
Original forest land (pre-Columbian):		
Temperate rainforest	7,300,000	18,000,000
Other native forests (uncertain)	22,700,000	56,000,000
Total	**30,000,000**	**74,000,000**
Areas presently forested:		
Protected forest land	1,400,000	3,400,000
Degraded forests	3,300,000	8,200,000
Commercially productive native forest	7,500,000	18,500,000
Other native forests (uncertain)	1,100,000	2,700,000
Plantations	1,700,000	4,200,000
Total	**15,000,000**	**37,000,000**

Source: P. Donoso, 1991, CONAF, 1992-93, & misc.

percent of all forest industry exports over the last decade.

As for native forests, a 1980 decree by the Agriculture Ministry implemented a new set of technical regulations that defined the 12 forest types currently recognized by CONAF. The decree also required companies to prepare a management plan that must be approved by CONAF prior to beginning a harvesting operation. Four logging methods are prescribed and standards applied that require at least as much land to be reforested as is cut over. Violations are subject to stiff fines (if enforced by the courts).

Today, management plans are a principal means of controlling forest exploitation. A plan is defined in the law as "regulating the rational use of renewable natural resources of a given plot of land, with the purpose of extracting the maximum benefit from said resources and securing, at the same time, their conservation, improvement and expansion."[64] If an approved plan is implemented, soils and other resources are, in theory, well protected. CONAF, however, is frequently criticized for not enforcing these plans or the regulations strictly enough.

Through the years, laws have been adopted that protect other amenities of the forest as well, such as wildlife and scenic beauty. Examples are the Hunting Act of 1929, the Convention for the Protection of Flora, Fauna and Scenic Beauty of the Americas in

FUNDACION DE SANTIAGO

12 de Febrero de 1541

1967, and the Convention on International Trade in Endangered Species in 1975. Individual tree species have also been protected in one form or another through decrees, including the quillay in 1938, ulmo and tineo restrictions in 1940, protection for the Chilean palm in 1941, and alerce and araucaria in 1976.

Finally, in 1984, the National System of Protected Wildlands was created and all national parks, monuments and reserves established since 1907 were included in the system. CONAF's goal is to eventually incorporate representative portions of all Chilean ecosystems. This requires, of course, that sizeable fragments of endangered ecosystems remain available for protection over the near term.

Despite a long history of public protection of forest resources in Chile, native forests may be as vulnerable to destruction today as they have ever been. Controls over logging activity are certainly more effective than they were in the distant past; however, many Chileans insist that the government is not doing enough. A big part of the problem may be a simple lack of staff to enforce existing regulations. The *siempreverde*, for example, is subject to significant limitations intended to keep soils from eroding once an area has been cut over. But local residents have reported that logging often takes place in conflict with approved management plans.

Standing atop Cerro Santa Lucia, Santiago's most famous hill, Pedro de Valdivia declares his founding of the city in 1541. A beautiful reproduction of this painting hangs in the Plaza de Armas Museum of History a few blocks from Santa Lucia. In that year, natives of the Mapocho River valley were overwhelmed by these steel-armoured warriors from afar and their labor helped build the city. Today, indigenous people are asking for the return of Santa Lucia as well as a number of other areas throughout Chile.
❦ Ken Wilcox

Eucalyptus trees overlook formerly wooded hills west of Temuco in Region IX. Pine and eucalyptus plantations are rapidly expanding, even to the point of crowding out some small traditional farms.

CODEFF is pushing for more reforestation, but with native species, not aliens.

❀ Peter McBride

Clearcutting is not permitted on steep slopes within certain forest types, and the introduction of non-native species is prohibited in other areas. Yet people complain that, again, enforcement is inadequate, forest plans are violated, and that as much as a third of all logging in native forests might be illegal. Protected species like araucaria and alerce are poached frequently, and though subject to fines in excess of the value of the timber, local courts have a history of reducing fines to a bare minimum, resulting in little or no deterrence to violators. The government has appropriated some additional funding to assist CONAF with enforcement, but mandatory penalties are also needed.

With the emergence of pine as a principal resource in Chile, most agree that all forest laws need to be revisited. Rapid growth in the industry and the substitution of native forests by plantations, combined with the public's growing concern for environmental quality and native forest ecosystems, have introduced new priorities into the long-term management of Chile's native forests. The situation becomes more urgent when one considers that wood chips are now being produced from pine, eucalyptus and native trees at record rates. Wood chip exports rose from virtually nothing in 1985 to more than 2.5 million tons in 1992. And the production of plantation timber is projected to double by the year 2000.[65]

New regulations are slowly being developed. In April, 1992, the Aylwin government submitted its proposal for a new forest law to Congress and a year-long debate was anticipated. The law would improve the management of native forests and provide incentives for reforestation with native species, but it would also allow the conversion of hundreds of thousands of hectares of "degraded" native forest to exotic species plantations. By 1995 the

A rare public protest in 1990 in front of CONAF headquarters in Santiago. The once-protected araucaria forests had been opened to logging in the late 1980s, raising the ire of those concerned with the future of this seriously depleted species. The Aylwin government reinstated the araucaria's Natural Monument status within weeks of the inauguration.
✿ Ken Wilcox

law had not yet been adopted and a new version submitted by the Frei government still languished in the Congress.

CODEFF has objected strongly to the conversions for several reasons. There is no clear definition of the term "degraded." It is not a biological term and only opens the door to excessive cutting. Native forests could be replaced on hillsides as steep as 30 degrees, a number that also lacks any basis in forest ecology. Instead, CODEFF has proposed that the legislation include funding for conservation and sustainable forestry practices, training for small landowners, outright prohibitions on chipping native woods or replacing them with exotic species, mandatory environmental impact assessment for large-scale projects, better access to information, and improved administration and enforcement.[66]

Industrialists argue that the old restrictions on native forest exploitation are sufficient and that Chileans ought to be more concerned with the economic benefits of large-scale exploitation. The industry has identified 7.5 million hectares of "potentially productive" native forest (an area larger than Ireland) it believes should be available for exploitation.

Prior to 1956, native forests provided virtually all commercial timber in Chile.[67] But now that pine is doing so well, the bigger companies are advocating conversion of large areas of native forests to plantations—the antithesis of Chile's rich and largely endemic floral diversity. Even without the conversions, at the rate trees are growing in Chile and world markets are expanding, the industry will likely be selling wood fiber at a premium well into the future.

Nations Within Nations

Indigenous people around the world are often immersed in non-native cultures, societies and nations that have little relevance to their own cultural identity or regional heritage. In Canada and elsewhere, native peoples have come to be known as "first nations," or those who occupied a particular region before the first whites arrived. As non-natives came to dominate society and the landscape, native people have struggled to secure their fundamental rights to self-determination, to be regarded as nations.

Similarly, native people in Chile have been squeezed from the land by settlers, forest exploiters, developers and others since the first Spaniards set foot there in the sixteenth century. Wars raged for more than three hundred years. Yet the largest indigenous group in Chile, the Mapuche, or "people of the land," were never defeated. Since their "pacification" in the 1880s, indigenous people have been subjected to an endless stream of broken promises, cultural oppression and more invasions. The effect has been to remove them further from the land that has sustained their lives and livelihoods for millennia.

In 1991, President Aylwin greeted several thousand Huilliches (one of several Mapuche tribes in southern Chile) to hear their appeal for a return of land that has been taken away. An indigenous leader, or "cacique," put it bluntly:

> We remain standing, together with our fight for the land which was ours before this country was called Chile. A Mapuche without land is not a Mapuche, which is why we are here before you now, to demand our right to the land which gives us our reason to live.[68]

In January 1993, a new indigenous law was passed by Congress that recognizes indigenous peoples' right to exist without discrimination. The law protects existing land holdings, and provides a small amount of funding to acquire land and to promote social and economic development. Some argue that the legislation does not go far enough in that it fails to recognize indigenous people as a separate people under the constitution.[69] Others agree, however, that the new law is a hopeful step toward resolving "first nation" struggles within the Chilean nation.

Lautaro, a young warrior-leader of the mid-1500s, is well known to most Chileans. He is credited with the cunning demise of the governor, Pedro de Valdivia in the early years of Spanish colonization.

❀ Peter McBride

Native people occupied the temperate rainforest coast of Chilean Patagonia for millennia, as illustrated in this work by a 19th century artist aboard Darwin's HMS Beagle. Below, the Beagle is greeted by canoes near Tierra del Fuego.

From the MEMOIRS of Pablo Neruda...

Under the volcanoes,
beside the snow-capped mountains,
among the huge lakes,
the fragrant, the silent, the tangled Chilean forest...
My feet sink down into the dead leaves, a fragile twig crackles,
the giant raulí trees rise in all their bristling height,
a bird from the cold jungle passes over, flaps its wings,
and stops in the sunless branches.
And then, from its hideaway, it sings like an oboe...
This is a vertical world: a nation of birds,
a plenitude of leaves...
an enormous spider covered with red hair stares up at me,
motionless, as huge as a crab...
A golden carabus beetle blows its mephitic breath at me,
as its brilliant rainbow disappears like lightning...
A decaying tree trunk: what a treasure!...
Black and blue mushrooms have given it ears,
red parasite plants have covered it with rubies,
other lazy plants have let it borrow their beards,
and a snake springs out of the rotted body like a sudden breath...
A gorge; below, the crystal water slides over granite and jasper...
A fox cuts through the silence like a flash,
sending a shiver through the leaves...
I have come out of that landscape,
that mud, that silence,
to roam, to go singing through the world.

From Memoirs, *by Pablo Neruda, Penguin Books, 1978.*

Part 3

Forest Conservation

SINCE THE ARRIVAL OF THE FIRST EUROPEANS in Chile nearly five centuries ago, huge areas of the country's forests have been dramatically transformed. Immense stands of low-elevation old-growth forest, an ancient temperate forest that rivaled even the classic groves of the Pacific Northwest is now degraded, unproductive second growth. After generations of burning and cutting, millions of hectares of forest have vanished altogether.

For the most part, people cleared these wild forests for honorable purposes: to open the land to farming, livestock grazing and other uses, and to obtain building lumber and fuelwood for heating, cooking and smelting. Yet, in the excitement of settling the land, homesteaders were responsible for setting countless fires that raged on for months at a time, destroying far more forest than was ever necessary to strike a good living. The leveling of whole forests was, ecologically, an all too familiar catastrophe — one of many that occurred throughout the New World after 1492. The situation would be much worse, however, had a few influential and visionary Chileans not had the foresight to protect some of the nation's original forests.

Araucaria at Nahuelbuta National Park, a 6,800 hectare reserve near Angol, established in 1939. ❀ Ken Wilcox

In spite of the great losses, forest conservation in Chile has a long history, from regulations of the early 1800s designed to protect forested commons to the establishment of the 107,000-hectare Galletué araucaria reserve and Pehuenche homeland at Quinquen in 1991. Chile was one of the first Latin American countries to officially designate national protected areas.

Federico Albert, a scientist-bureaucrat from Germany, is credited with what may be the oldest forest preserve on the South American continent: Chile's Malleco National Reserve set aside in 1907. Vicente Pérez Rosales National Park is the oldest national park, established in 1925.[70] Many other protected areas were added in the 1960s and 1970s. By the 1980s, a National System of Protected Wildlands had been created to help preserve some of

the nation's unique environments as well as species, genetic and ecosystem diversity throughout Chile.

Ecosystem values are a major criterion for establishing preservation priorities. CONAF officials, as well as other concerned Chileans, have strived to protect not only those places with scenic grandeur and outstanding recreation potential, but lands containing scarce ecosystems and critical habitat for sensitive wildlife species. The National System of Protected Wildlands administered by CONAF is also proactive in the sense that an overall objective of the program is to include representative portions of all known ecosystems in Chile *before* they become severely threatened. Intact ecosystems and biological diversity (*biodiversity*) will continue to be major considerations as new areas are identified for preservation.

Olivillo, canelo and arrayán are principal tree species inhabiting Fray Jorge National Park, an unusual mountaintop rainforest near La Serena. The forest is perched above the desert, sustained by humid air rolling off the Pacific Ocean and condensing into fog and rain as it rises. In the park's lower elevations, cactus and guayacán are common, in stark contrast to the high forest. Strangely, the rainforest is similar in composition to parts of the Valdivian Rainforest 1,000 kilometers to the south.
❀ Ken Wilcox

3.1 Protected Wildlands

In 1984, ACT 18,362 CREATED THE *National System of Protected Wildlands,* a comprehensive program that incorporated almost all of the national parks, reserves and natural monuments in existence at the time.[71] The Act's principal objectives were explained in Article 1:

- *To maintain wildlands noteworthy for their uniqueness or representation of the country's natural ecological diversity...*
- *To secure the continuity of evolutionary processes, animal migrations, patterns of genetic flow...*
- *To maintain and improve wild flora and fauna resources and to rationalize their utilization...*

By May of 1991, 13,832,184.1 hectares, or about 18 percent of the country, was included in the system. A total of 80 units had been established (several more have been added, including two new northern national parks in 1995. Chile is seventh in the world and third in the Americas (behind Ecuador and Belize) in the *percentage* of the nation that has been protected.[72] The numbers are impressive, but they can also be misleading.

Most of the protected areas are concentrated in the far south—Regions XI (Aisén) and XII (Magallanes)—where total biodiversity is much more limited than in Region X (Los Lagos). Forests in the far south are subject to difficult growing conditions like inhospitable climate and poor soils—which is not to say these forests should not be protected. With the exception of Tierra del Fuego, Chilean Patagonia is one of the largest protected coastal forest regions on the planet. Yet to the north in Region X, the rich diversity of the Valdivian Rainforest is poorly protected. The mature lenga and coihue forests on the island of Tierra del Fuego are conspicuously absent from the protected wildlands system.

As it stands now, 85 percent of all protected areas in Chile are located in the southern third of the nation, from 44° South latitude and beyond. Most of the balance is in the far north, in the Andean *altiplano* and dry deserts of Region I (Tarapacá). As a

National System
of Protected Wildlands (1991)

	Sites	Hectares
National Parks	30	8,358,367.0
National Reserves	39	5,459,344.8
Natural Monuments	11	14,472.3
Total:	**80**	**13,832,184.1**

Regional Distribution
(% of Total)

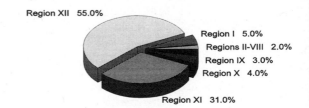

Region XII 55.0%

Region I 5.0%
Regions II-VIII 2.0%
Region IX 3.0%
Region X 4.0%

Region XI 31.0%

5% of the total is private land.
Source: CONAF, 1991

result, less than 10 percent of all protected areas are reasonably accessible to the average Chilean.

Protected areas are most lacking in the central regions, where close to 90 percent of the population lives. In Regions VII (Maule) and VIII (Bío-Bío) the lack of publicly owned land and the replacement of native forests by pine plantations during the second half of this century guarantee major difficulties in establishing large new protected areas in central Chile. The only sizeable natural areas that might be added to the system are located high in the mountains, on steep slopes, and in wetland areas. Central Chile was, after all, the first region to be settled by the Spanish and first to be privatized through land grant schemes. Nevertheless, CONAF and university experts have compiled inventories of high-priority sites worth protecting. All are privately owned.

Not only are protected areas poorly distributed around the country, most wildlands are unforested and largely composed of rock, ice, moorland, tundra and desert. Estimates of protected forest land in Chile range from 1.3 million to over 6 million hectares (CONAF assumed in the past that roughly half of the 13.8 million hectares of protected land in the country is forested; however, no reliable figures are available to confirm this).[73]

Although all twelve forest types are found in the protected areas system, most are not sufficiently represented. In the south, for example, the *siempreverde* forest is one of the least protected. It contains the richest diversity of species and ecosystems in all of Chile's forests, yet is most vulnerable to logging and development. As the most biologically complex of the twelve forest types, the forest is noted for its wide variety of tangled plant communities, distinct species and ecological characteristics that differ significantly from one part of the forest to the next.

It is not enough to set aside two or three small areas in the coastal range (as is presently the case) and presume that the largest contiguous region of *siempreverde* or broadleaved evergreen forest in Chile is adequately protected. It simply is not. Furthermore, virtually the entire *siempreverde* is within Chile's coastal temperate rainforest, a scarce forest environment worldwide and the largest in the southern hemisphere. Much more research is needed to better understand the composition and distribution of this unique rainforest.

Other forest types in the far south, lenga and Magellanic coihue in particular, are much better protected (except on Tierra del Fuego). The alerce, araucaria and Chilean palm forest types are well protected only in the sense that all three species are off limits to cutting. That is no guarantee, however, that poaching does not occur (it does) or that the present range of each is sufficient to sustain its long-term viability or that of any associated plant communities. The araucaria and alerce forests

"Every living species is a unique national and world asset which, if extinct, becomes absolutely irrecuperable, entailing an economic, ecologic, scientific and educational loss."
—Iván Benoit,
CONAF [1989]

Chile's Protected Wildlands

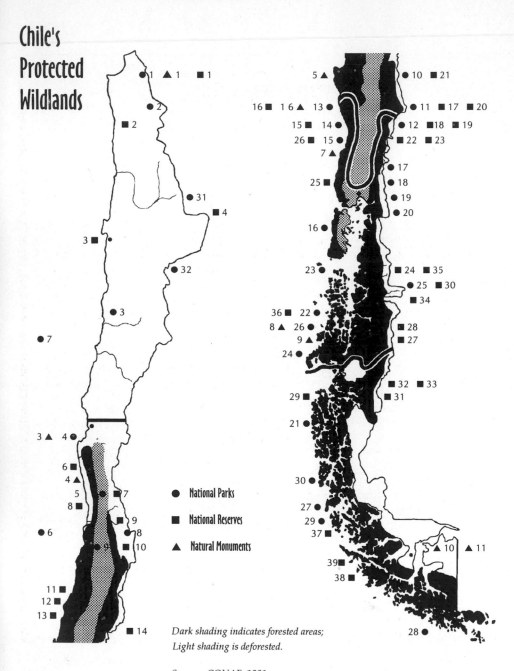

● National Parks

■ National Reserves

▲ Natural Monuments

Dark shading indicates forested areas;
Light shading is deforested.

Source: CONAF, 1991

Protected Wildlands of Chile

● National Parks

1 Lauca
2 Volcán Isluga
3 Pan de Azúcar
4 Bosque Fray Jorge
5 La Campana
6 Archipiélago de Juan Fernández
7 Rapa Nui
8 El Morado
9 Palmas de Cocalán
10 Laguna del Laja
11 Conguillío
12 Huerquehue
13 Nahuelbuta
14 Tolhuaca
15 Villarrica
16 Chiloé
17 Puyehue
18 Vicente Pérez Rosales
19 Alerce Andino
20 Hornopirén
21 Bernardo O'Higgings
22 Isla Guamblin
23 Isla Magdalena
24 Laguna San Rafael
25 Queulat
26 Río Simpson
27 Alberto de Agostini
28 Cabo de Hornos
29 Pali Aike
30 Torres del Paine
31 Licanbur (1995)
32 Llullaillaco (1995)

■ National Reserves

1 Las Vicuñas
2 Pampa del Tamarugal
3 La Chimba
4 Los Flamencos
5 Pinguino de Humboldt
6 Las Chinchillas
7 Río Blanco
8 Lago Peñuelas
9 Río Clarillo
10 Río de Los Cipreses
11 Federico Albert
12 Laguna Torca
13 Los Ruiles
14 Ñuble
15 Isla Mocha
16 Ralco
17 Alto Bío-Bío
18 China Muerta
19 Malalcahuello
20 Malleco
21 Nalcas
22 Gualletué
23 Villarrica
24 Lago Palena
25 Llanquihue
26 Valdivia
27 Cerro Castillo
28 Coihaique
29 Katalalixar
30 Lago Carlota
31 Lago Cochrane
32 Lago General Carrera
33 Lago Jeinimeni
34 Lago Las Torres
35 Lago Roselot
36 Las Guaitecas
37 Alacalufes
38 Laguna Parrillar
39 Magallanes

▲ Natural Monuments

1 Salar de Surire
2 La Portada
3 Pichasca
4 Isla Cachagua
5 Contulmo
6 Cerro Ñielol
7 Alerce Costero
8 Dos Lagunas
9 Cinco Hermanas
10 Los Pinguinos
11 Laguna de los Cisnes

Source: CONAF, 1991

occupy, at most, 300,000 hectares each (Regions IX and X), an area smaller than the state of Rhode Island in the U.S.

All of the country's remaining forest types are only marginally represented in the protected areas system. Thus, Chile's exceptional diversity is not as well represented as it might appear at first glance. Of the 83 floristic formations (loosely, ecosystems) identified in Chile, only 54 (65%) are found within the system.[74] At least one-third are unprotected.

In terms of individual species, CONAF estimated in 1989 that 90 percent of native tree species (along with 68 percent of mammals and 61 percent of birds) were represented to one degree or another.[75] Complete species inventories for protected areas are rare to nonexistent, particularly for invertebrates and inferior plants (e.g. lichens, algae, fungi). Although a brief summary of resident fauna and flora is available for most of the country's parks, reserves and monuments, a thorough assessment of protected native forest ecosystems has never been conducted.

Even though protection is incomplete and disproportionate nationally, the situation is expected to improve. Since 1980, the government's primary goal in administering the National System of Protected Wildlands has been to protect biological diversity. Between 1980 and 1988, nine new reserves and four national parks were designated. All included ecosystems that were not previously protected. Several more had been added by 1995. Others have been targeted for action and, for some, negotiations are underway with public and private landowners to provide interim protection until public acquisition becomes feasible.

Conserving native forests is critically important to the future of Chilean ecosystems. As noted earlier, over half of all plant species in Chile are *endemic*: plants that do not occur naturally anywhere else in the world. A good number of them are found in forests. In fact, all major Chilean forest species are endemic to the Andean region and nearly all are found principally on the Chilean side of the range. For example, southern beech *(Nothofagus)* are among Chile's most abundant and widespread trees. Of the ten species present, four are endemic. Other trees, like the two belloto species, lleuque (one of the *podocarp* conifers), and the very rare queule, ruil and pitao trees are all endemics, as are the Chilean palms, the southernmost palms in the world.

Trees that are unique to Chile have all been substantially depleted and none presently occur in commercially productive populations. Yet all native trees, not just endemics, are vital to the health and integrity of forest ecosystems. All are deserving of some measure of protection in their natural range.

It should be noted that there are protected area classifications other than parks, reserves and monuments. These include *Reservas de Interés Científico* (Scientific Interest Reserves), *Areas de Protección Turistica* (Tourist Protected Areas), and *Reservas de la Biosfera* (Biosphere Reserves). Such areas may also be in some other protected status, or may be privately owned where management for preservation might be arranged voluntarily by mutual agreement between CONAF and the landowner. This cooperative approach has worked well for some of the smallest sites and will likely be an important tool in protecting similar lands in the future. Significant private conservation initiatives also occur, such as Parque Pumalin in Region X (*see p. 28 and sidebar*→), and the Cañi Forest Sanctuary in Region IX (*p. 82*).

Finally, one of the more complex protected area issues concerns their potential undoing by political forces that may not be entirely committed to long-term stewardship or, in the extreme case, to any protection within the system. Hornopirén National Park southeast of Puerto Montt shrank substantially following a boundary dispute with a large timber company in the 1980s. Another, Lago Galletué National Park in the headwaters of the

"The biotic richness of an area is the degree of endemism of the biota."

H. A. Mooney,
BIODIVERSITY [1988]

The Law of Private Parks

In 1994, a new law was enacted which recognizes the right of private entities to establish national parks, monuments and reserves in Chile. The Law of Private Parks, a component of the 1994 Environmental Law, encourages protection of all ecosystem types in the country. Land protected in this way must comply with several criteria to ensure the validity of such efforts. Private initiatives like Parque Pumalin and the Cañi Forest Sanctuary are exemplary and crucial considering the accelerated pace of resource exploitation in Chile and limited government funds to acquire land. The government estimates the cost of acquiring suitable reserves of currently unprotected ecosystems at a half-billion dollars.

Bío-Bío River, was dissolved altogether and returned to private hands in the 1970s.[76] The two sites contained outstanding examples of alerce and araucaria forest, respectively, some of which has since been destroyed.

Prior to the 1960s, it was not unheard of for some areas to be "protected" after they had already been logged. Mining occurs within national parks, and large areas of native forest are vulnerable to open pit mining. These and other potential difficulties cannot easily be predicted. On the upside, political actions which contradict the preservation and stewardship purposes of the protected areas system may be less likely now that Chile has returned to its long-standing democratic traditions and a popularly elected government.

The Cañi Forest Sanctuary, located in the humid araucaria forests near Pucón, is an outstanding example of what can be achieved by private individuals and organizations determined to protect native forest diversity in Chile. The sanctuary's 480 hectares are home to foxes, pudu, puma, rodents, bats, hummingbirds, Andean condors, ibis, Magellanic woodpeckers and owls among other wildlife. The Cañi also supports an ongoing environmental education program for school teachers. Originally purchased for preservation by a concerned resident of the area, the reserve has become a milestone project for the Lahuen Foundation, thanks to the support of the Weeden Foundation, Patagonia, Inc., Esprit-Chile, AFI and the World Parks Endowment Fund.

❦ Dan Dancer

3.2 Biodiversity Conservation

IN RECENT YEARS, THE CONSERVATION of biological diversity has become one of the world's leading crusades for the environment. It is easy to understand why.

Living resources are utilized or consumed by every human being on the planet. They are bought and sold in the world marketplace and contribute to every nation's economy. Native plants, animals and the products derived from them are sources of food, shelter, clothing, tools, medicine and much more. Even domesticated livestock and food crops can be traced to their wild origins; several varieties of the potato, South America's gift to Europe in the sixteenth century, may have their origin in the Chilean rainforest.

Surely new products will emerge in the future as we discover new ways to utilize living resources. Yet when a plant or animal species is extirpated from its natural range or becomes extinct, its known or potential value to human society is lost forever.

More than 60 percent of all modern medicines originally came from native plants. Medicinal plants growing wild in Chile are widely used in health care and contribute millions of dollars to the national economy each year. Compounds derived from the leaves of boldo trees, for example, are used in the professional treatment of liver ailments and digestive problems. Canelo bark is high in Vitamin C and was used long ago on sailing ships to prevent scurvy. The tree is also thought to be useful in treating cancer. The Mapuche people utilize the sacred canelo and a substantial number of other native plants for traditional treatments and remedies. No one can guess how many plants unique to Chilean forests—or native forests worldwide—may promise human health benefits in the future.

In the Pacific Northwest, derivatives of the bark and needles of the Pacific yew tree received wide attention recently as a potential cure for ovarian cancer and leukemia. Over the last century, yew trees were cut and discarded by the millions because science had not adequately investigated the tree's value to medicine. But now that it promises a new cure for cancer, we

Identifying mosses in the high meadows above Huinay in the northern reaches of Chilean Patagonia.

☀ Ken Wilcox

The Copihue, Chile's National Flower

The distinct, vibrant red, trumpet-shaped flower of the Chilean rainforest, the copihue (*Lapageria rosea*), figures prominently in Chilean culture and in the legends of the Mapuche people. Hummingbirds distribute the pollen from flowers that bloom from a shaded vine in the forest canopy. An edible fruit appears in the fall.

The copihue was recognized as Chile's national flower in 1977 and its image adorns a multitude of commercial products. Paintings and photographs of the flower brighten the halls of homes and public buildings throughout the country.

Although a number of varieties have been propagated and are widely planted in gardens, deforestation, soil erosion and perhaps climate change have significantly reduced the natural range of the copihue. It is now considered to be in some danger of extinction.[77]

find very few yew trees still standing. For all we know, the canelo is another "yew tree" of crucial importance to human health. Its habitat is the Chilean rainforest.

Every plant species alive today contains a different arrangement of chemical compounds, many of which could prove extremely valuable to the future well-being of human society. It is in everyone's interest worldwide to protect the diversity of life that already exists.

Medicinal values are only one of the many reasons to safeguard biodiversity. The health and integrity of entire ecosystems may be threatened with the loss of any single species. Such a loss may bring a subtle or abrupt interruption to the natural dynamics at work within plant and animal communities. If the impact is great, equilibrium of the ecosystem is upset and other species may suffer. The mattoral scrublands of central Chile are a testament to the disruptive consequences of indiscriminate clearing within a once-thriving woodland ecosystem. The protected status of araucaria, alerce, Chilean palm, queule, belloto, ruil, pitao and others are all reminders that human activity can be seriously detrimental to ecosystems.

In our untethered zeal to use and develop nature's wealth, we are quick to overlook ecological values, as well as what some view as the universal right of all species to carry on, to sustain themselves and their offspring in a dignified way. A few species are already extinct in Chile and many others are in danger of disappearing. Lacking strong environmental policies and adequate safeguards, coupled with massive deterioration of the ozone layer above southern Chile and the prospects for global warming, uncounted species within Chilean forests may face severe consequences during the next century.

From a global perspective, what makes the Chilean situation unique? How have native forests, the ancient ones especially, come to be regarded as something special among the vast forests of the Green Continent? There are clear answers to both questions.

It is well established that Chile's diverse flora and fauna and high degree of endemism come from a number of unique factors. For one, Chile is 4,300 kilometers long from north to south, bounded by the Pacific Ocean to the west, arid deserts to the north and by the high rugged crest of the Andes to the east. It is difficult for species to move into or out of Chile and has been for millions of years. Consequently, plants and animals have evolved in relative isolation from the rest of the world—South America included. By default, almost every river valley cuts through the lowlands from east to west, further isolating species, populations and gene pools from potential habitats in adjoining regions.

Long before Chile became Chile, the South American continent was part of the supercontinent Gondwanaland. The Nothofagus, Podocarp and Araucaria forests that left their fossilized imprints in Australasia and Antarctica more than 100 million years ago are survived by contemporary Chilean forests that have evolved in isolation from the rest of the world literally for eons.

As the most successful inhabitants of a diversity of forested and non-forested environments, Chilean native species have become vibrant mosaics of interdependent organisms distinct from all others on the planet.

These mosaics of biodiversity can be discussed at three levels: *ecosystem*, *species*, and *genetic diversity*. The first generally refers to the bigger picture, that is, the variety of distinct plant and animal communities that can be described for a particular region. The second suggests the array of individual types of organisms that inhabit an ecosystem. The third level of diversity looks at variations among populations and individuals within the same species.

Ecosystem Diversity

Unlike other South American countries, virtually all Chile's forests are temperate—not tropical. In Chile, the greatest diversity and the most productive terrestrial ecosystems occur in the form of temperate rainforest, a flourishing broadleaf evergreen forest that is actually more closely related to cloudforests in the tropics than to other temperate rainforests in the northern hemisphere. Temperate forests occur as far south as Tierra del Fuego and well to the north of Santiago, especially in the higher elevations. Forests that are not truly temperate are those inhabiting the northern extent of Chile's forested lowlands where a drier subtropical climate predominates.

Nearer the equator, warm wet tropical ecosystems are thought to be the most diverse overall. Yet life's diversity in the middle latitudes cannot be lightly regarded. In Mediterranean climates like that of central Chile, natural diversity can be rich in endemic species. Such biogeoclimatic regions, with mild moist winters and warm dry summers, occur in only five places in the world. Four of them merge with cool wet regions that support the bulk of the world's temperate rainforests. Species diversity and biomass are impressive in all of them. Great ancient forests like the Valdivian Rainforest in southern Chile and the Olympic Rainforest in the Pacific Northwest are home to numbers of vertebrate, invertebrate and vascular plant species measured in the thousands. Despite the similarities in climate, latitude and

A bandurria (Theristicus caudatus) with its distinctive bill and markings flies over Chilean Patagonia.
❀ Peter McBride

coastal mountain topography, American rainforests and those of New Zealand and Tasmania are each comprised of entirely different plant communities. (The rainforests of Chile and New Zealand are similarly dominated by southern beech, but the species are not the same.)

Throughout Earth's middle latitudes, temperate forests at one time covered roughly the same area as tropical forests. Prior to the development of agriculture, it is estimated that each type of forest covered about 17 to 18 million square kilometers or 12 percent of the planet's land area. For several thousand years forests shrank substantially from the effects of agriculture, timber harvest and the development of cities. Closed-canopy temperate forests worldwide have declined by a third or more.

Only recently has deforestation in the tropics assumed major proportions.[78] As a result of tropical deforestation, a continuing decline in forest cover is projected for Latin America as a whole over the next three decades.[79] Temperate forests, on the other hand, are actually increasing — that is, if single-species tree "plantations" are considered synonymous with "forest." Primary forests, the ultimate source of natural diversity in Chile, British Columbia, Siberia and elsewhere, are declining at a rapid rate.

While nearly all Chilean forests can be classified as temperate, the term is far too broad to convey the uniqueness of each forest type, ecosystem or floristic formation.

In *A Biogeographical Classification for Terrestrial Environments*,[80] terrestrial earth is divided into eight *realms* and 227 *biogeographical provinces*. Three of the eight realms are present in Chile: *Oceanic*, *Antarctic* and *Neotropical* (which includes essentially everything from the State of Florida and Baja, Mexico, south to Tierra del Fuego). Of the 47 provinces found in the Neotropical Realm, 12 occur in Chile,[81] one each on Rapa Nui (Easter Island) and Juan Fernández Islands, one in the Antarctic Territory and nine on the mainland. Four of the 12 provinces are unique to Chile.

In 1983, Chilean biologist Rodolfo Gajardo departed somewhat from the Uvardy system and proposed that eight *ecological regions*, 17 *ecological subregions*, and 83 *floristic formations* exist within Chile, excluding off-shore islands and the giant slice of Antarctic Territory claimed by the Chilean government. (Others have proposed similar classification systems. UNESCO mapped all vegetation of South America in the 1970s, identifying 103 floristic formations based on climate and soil types — the two most influential factors in vegetation origin. Cabrera *et al.* [1975] and Hueck [1978] have suggested other approaches as well. The Gajardo work is most widely accepted.) Chilean native forest floristic formations are listed on page 13. These formations and the animal life that inhabits them are, roughly speaking, ecosystems. It is important to keep in mind, however, that using this system to define a particular ecosystem for study or preservation is not always easy since a variety of plant and animal communities can occur within any one formation.

Distinct floristic formations or ecosystems can be found in the barren deserts, salt lakes, scrublands and grasslands of the north; in the sclerophyllous forests, rich shrublands and highland southern beech forests of central Chile; in the temperate rainforest region of southern Chile; in the glacial tundra, moorlands (peat swamps or *turberas*) and inland mixed subpolar forests in the far south; and on most of the larger off-shore islands. Within each ecosystem, individual species have evolved to take advantage of unique habitat opportunities. In general terms, the more complex the ecosystem, the greater the diversity of species.

Species Diversity

Species diversity for both plants and animals largely results from the diversity of habitats that can be successfully occupied. Habitat, in turn, is influenced by climate and soils, both of which

High above the northern fiords of Chilean Patagonia, an AFI expedition member views one of the richest, wettest temperate rainforest regions on Earth.
❀ Craig Marks

vary tremendously over changes in latitude, elevation and slope aspect. In Chile, annual rainfall averages range from zero in the driest parts of the Atacama Desert to at least 6,000 mm in the rainforest region.[82] The relative abundance of sunlight and shade are also highly variable, as are day/night temperature ranges, extremes and seasonal norms. It is no surprise then that habitat and species diversity are so great in a country whose land and climate are as multifarious as Chile's.

The greatest concentration of species in the world is found within the Neotropical Realm to which most of Chile's forests belong. Neotropical species worldwide are so numerous and vastly uncatalogued that scientists can only guess at their numbers, probably in excess of 10 million. Biologist E. O. Wilson estimates there are as many as 30 million living species in the world including, perhaps, more than five million insects.[83] Of that number, a third or more probably inhabit Neotropic regions. Estimates are difficult to make since only 1.5 million species have been identified worldwide — and half of them are insects. Another 250,000 are superior plants (vascular and bryophytes) and 41,000 are vertebrates. The rest are mostly invertebrates, fungi, algae and a host of microorganisms.[84]

In Chile, Gajardo counted 4,758 superior plant species in 190 families and 965 genera.[85] Of the total, 2,698 species are considered endemic, 1,632 are native plants also found outside the country, and 428 are introduced species. As many as 125 tree species have been reported including tree-sized ferns and cacti.[86] (Marticorena and Quezada in 1983 counted 5,215 vascular plants and bryophytes in 192 families and 1,032 genera. A total of 157 are pteridophytes, 17 are gymnosperms, 3,996 are dicots and 1,045 are monocots.[87])

Of all the native plants that grow in Chile, 69 species are classified as either endangered, vulnerable to extinction, or rare.[88] Sixteen of them are trees. At least 50 other plant species, including at least 22 trees, are considered endangered, vulnerable or rare from a regional standpoint (which means that certain populations are in need of conservation even though the species itself may be faring better elsewhere in the country). Botanists are concerned about the long-term viability of a few additional species but not enough information is available to properly classify them. Others, still, could be downgraded.

These numbers are significant: there are at least 38 species of Chilean trees that are listed either regionally or nationally as endangered, vulnerable or rare. The bulk of them occur in central Chile, particularly Regions VI, VII, VIII and IX.

Endangered trees are also found in Regions IV (radal), V (roble-pellín), VIII (belloto del sur, queule and pitao) and IX (pitao). Species conservation in Region X is of particular

With wings spanning nine feet or more, an Andean condor glides effortlessly near Laguna del Laja National Park in the Bío-Bío Region, east of Concepción.
❧ Ken Wilcox

concern due to the presence of six trees that are listed as vulnerable or rare: araucaria, alerce, cordilleran cypress, boldo, huillipatagua and lleuque.

Chilean forests provide habitats for an exceptional variety of animals. Wildlife diversity includes 124 native and 15 introduced mammals, plus 6 others that are suspected but not yet confirmed.[89] There are 439 birds in Chile, 84 reptiles, 39 amphibians and 44 fresh water fishes. Many are endemic species. Unfortunately, not all of them occur in healthy populations.

On the list of *endangered* Chilean wildlife there are 15 mammals, 10 birds, one reptile, 6 amphibians and 18 fish.[90] One mammal (Riesco tuco-tuco) and one bird (eskimo curlew) are thought to be extinct. *Vulnerable* species include another 15

Region VII: Chile's Most Endangered

The nation's highest concentration of endangered trees—six species—is in Region VII (Maule), in central Chile. Protected areas are also more severely lacking here than anywhere else in the country. Four of the six endangered trees are not represented at all in the National System of Protected Wildlands. The other two, ruil and pitao, are found only in Los Ruiles National Reserve, which at 45 hectares is the tiniest reserve in the system.

Clearly, biodiversity conservation is in a bleak state in Region VII. For CODEFF and CONAF, the problem has been a priority concern for many years.

Cordilleran cypress.
✿ Adriana Hoffmann

Endangered, Vulnerable & Rare Trees of Chile

Nationally Listed Species

Endangered

		Origin	Location
Southern belloto	(Beilschmiedia berteroana)	Endemic	VII, VIII
Queule	(Gomortega keule)	Endemic	VII, VIII
Ruil	(Nothofagus alessandrii)	Endemic	VII
Pitao	(Pitavia punctata)	Endemic	VII, VIII, IX

Vulnerable

Araucaria	(Araucaria araucana)	Chile & Argentina	VIII, IX, X
Cordilleran cypress	(Austrocedrus chilensis)	Chile & Argentina	V, M, VI, VII, VIII, IX, X
Northern belloto	(Beilschmiedia miersii)	Endemic	V, M, VI
Tayú	(Dasyphyllum excelsum)	Endemic	V, VI, VII
Alerce	(Fitzroya cupressoides)	Chile & Argentina	X
Chilean palm	(Jubaea chilensis)	Endemic	IV, V, M, VI, VII
Hualo	(Nothofagus glauca)	Endemic	M, VI, VII, VIII
Huala	(Nothofagus leonii)	Endemic	VII, VIII
Guayacán	(Porlieria chilensis)	Endemic	IV, V, M, VI

Rare

Huillipatagua	(Citronella mucronata)	Endemic	IV, V, M, VI, VII, VIII, IX, X
Guindo santo	(Eucryphia glutinosa)	Endemic	VII, VIII, IX
Lleuque	(Prumnopytis andina)	Endemic	VII, VIII, IX, X

Source: CONAF, 1989.

mammals, 32 birds, 13 reptiles, 9 amphibians and 23 fishes. *Rare* species include 12 mammals, 12 birds, 18 reptiles, 10 amphibians and one fish. All are recognized internationally as species of concern, and most are subject to restrictions on capture, possession and international trade.

A number of programs are underway in Chile with the aim of restoring sparse populations to sustainable levels, such as the reintroduction of alpaca (domesticated) and guanaco into suitable habitat areas for commercial wool production. Long ago, millions of guanaco roamed both forested and unforested landscapes but only 10,000 remained in the 1960s due to their senseless killing by hunters seeking the animal's exquisite wool. The expensive wool will now be collected from live animals. Although not truly domesticated, they hold much promise as livestock, generating far less impact on soils and vegetation than cows or sheep.

A captive breeding program has been established at the University of Concepción for the tiny pudu deer. The deer is dependent on temperate rainforest habitat and is particularly

Endangered, Vulnerable & Rare Trees of Chile

Regionally Listed Species

Endangered

		Origin	Location
Radal	(Lomatia hirsuta)	Chile, Argentina, Peru & Ecuador	IV
Roble	(Nothofagus obliqua-macrocarpa)	Chile	V (Vulnerable in M & VI)
Tineo	(Weinmannia trichosperma)	Chile & Argentina	VII
Short-leaved mañío	(Saxegothaea conspicua)	Chile & Argentina	VII

Vulnerable

		Origin	Location
Lingue	(Persea lingue)	Endemic	IX
Laurel	(Laurelia sempervirens)	Endemic	VI, VII
Boldo	(Peumus boldus)	Endemic	X
Peumo	(Cryptocarya alba)	Endemic	M (Rare in IX)
Patagua	(Crinodendron patagua)	Endemic	VII
Olivillo	(Aextoxicon punctatum)	Chile & Argentina	IV, V, M
Quillay	(Quillaja saponaria)	Endemic	IV
Temu	(Blepharocalix cruckshanksii)	Endemic	V, VI
Raulí	(Nothofagus alpina)	Chile & Argentina	VII, IX
Canelo	(Drimys winteri)	Chile & Argentina	XII

Rare

		Origin	Location
Petra	(Myrceugenia exsucca)	Chile & Argentina	VI
Notro	(Embothrium coccineum)	Chile & Argentina	VII
Sauco del diablo	(Pseudopanax laetevirens)	Chile & Argentina	VII
Pelú	(Sophora microphylla)	Chile & New Zealand	VII
Ñirre	(Nothofagus antarctica)	Chile & Argentina	VII
Lenga	(Nothofagus pumilio)	Chile & Argentina	VII
Prickly-leaved mañío	(Podocarpus nubigena)	Chile & Argentina	IX
Fuinque	(Lomatia ferruginea)	Chile & Argentina	XII

Source: CONAF, 1989

vulnerable to disturbance by humans. A giant by comparison, the endangered huemul or Southern Andean deer has benefitted from strategic habitat protection measures in recent years, but remains in extreme danger of extinction (*see p. 94*).

Chiloé National Park officials have achieved some success in conserving their own pudu populations and recently began a similar effort oriented to endangered marine mammals, including otters and sea lions along the island's rainforest coast. Some effort has also gone into protecting habitat for the endangered tricahue parrot. As few as three thousand remain following a long history of deforestation and predation by humans and rodents.

As might be expected from Chile's physical isolation from the rest of the continent, endemic vertebrates are more highly concentrated here than in Latin America as a whole.[91] Several mammals are either endemic or are found only in Chilean and Argentine forests. These include (among others) a few rodents, two marsupials, river and sea-going otters, a fox, cat and two deer, the huemul and the pudu, tiniest true deer in the world.

Insects and other forest invertebrates are as unique as the rest of Chile's diversity of life. Flies and beetles—most of them innocuous—are among the most abundant insect families in Chilean forests, though poorly inventoried. Entomologists in Chile and elsewhere would like to see that situation changed.

In the Valdivian Rainforest, a surprising population of stoneflies caught the attention of entomologist David Herbst during a 1991 research expedition sponsored by Ancient Forest International. Stoneflies are among the oldest living species of insects, one of the first with wings. Interestingly, they are not good fliers. Since they cannot travel far, their populations are often isolated and endemic. The oldest known families of stoneflies are found in the forests of southern Chile. Herbst describes these remarkable insects and their habitat this way:

> *This area is a climatic and ecological remnant of Gondwanaland... in this rainforest so similar to its ancestral home, this relict lineage of insects is thriving. For an entomologist, it is as if there were a place, deep in remote forests isolated by mountains that rose from the sea, where a race of dinosaurs still lived.*[92]

Pudu, the world's tiniest true deer. This elusive creature of southern Chile's humid forests stands just 15 inches tall. Hunters, dogs and habitat loss have taken a toll on this beautiful animal.
❀ Ken Wilcox

The population and distribution of insects are not at the top of many lists for near-term research funding, nor for other arthropods (like centipedes and spiders) or annelids (earthworms). As we learn more about the intricate web of life that makes up a forest, we begin to recognize that even the tiniest creatures are critical to the larger scheme. All wildlife, great or small, should be presumed to be important players in Chilean ecosystems.

The lack of funding to support a comprehensive and continuing research program in Chile is a major impediment to gaining a more complete understanding of the nation's floral and faunal diversity. Basic field surveys and computer data base compilations are still high priorities among the scientific and academic communities. Data systems could benefit not only the wise management of ecosystems, they could help ensure that commercial and subsistence use of living resources is sustainable over the long term. Currently, the only notable data base in the country is one of superior plants at the University of Concepción's Laboratory of Botany. Considering just the economic role of forest resources, much more research funding is warranted.

Endangered, Vulnerable & Rare Mammals of Chilean Forests

Endangered
Long-snout rat-opossum *(Rhyncholestes raphanurus)*
Maulean coruro *(Spalacopus cyanus maulinus)*
Tierra del fuego culpeo fox *(Canis culpaeus lycoides)*
Southern river otter *(Lutra provocax)*

Colocolo *(Felis colocola)*
Geoffroy's cat *(Felis geoffroyi)*
Austral spotted cat *(Felis guigna)*
Huemul (southern Andean deer)
  (Hippocamelus bisulcus)

Vulnerable
Mountain viscacha *(Lagidium viscacia)*
Bridge's degu *(Octodon bridgesi)*
Coastal degu *(Octodon lunatus)*
Chiloé fox *(Canis fulvipes)*

Southern Sea Otter *(Lutra felina)*
Puma *(Felis concolor)*
Guanaco *(Lama guanicoe)*
Southern pudu *(Pudu pudu)*

Rare
Chiloé colocolo opossum *(Dromiciops australis gliroides)*
Valdivian mole-mouse *(Geoxis valdivianus)*

Great rock-rat
  (Aconaemys fuscusporteri)

Source: CONAF, 1989

Genetic Diversity

Scientists know little about genetic diversity within Chilean species populations, with the exception of a few domestic animals, food crops, and non-food plants. Most genetic research is supported by the agricultural sector, which relies on about 30 genera of native plants and their relatives to keep the industry thriving. A good share of the attention has focused on potatoes.

A few wildlife species such as vicuña, guanaco and puma (cougar or mountain lion) have been studied for morphological and genetic differences among populations. CONAF has made an effort to conserve morphological variability through the protection of different populations of endangered wildlife species. Their efforts have included several mammals, namely the huemul *(Hippocamelus bisulcus)*, taruca or Northern Andean deer *(H. antisensis)*, vicuña *(Vicugna vicugna)*, guanaco *(Lama guanicoe)* and chinchilla *(Chinchilla laniger)*; and birds like the suri *(Pterocnemia pennata)*, the tricahue parrot *(Cyanoliseous patagonus)* and the black-necked swan *(Cygnus melancoriphus)*.

The work has led to some positive developments. Vicuña populations increased dramatically from about 1,000 in 1973 to 7,900 in 1980 and then to 22,714 by 1988. The number of guanaco

The Endangered Huemul

The huemul, a large Andean deer native to Chile and a national symbol of the Chilean wilderness, has been in danger of extinction for generations. Not only is this docile animal easy prey for poachers, its numbers have declined substantially as a result of habitat destruction. The huemul depends on native forests for its survival and reproduction, forests that are steadily disappearing due to intentional fires and excessive cutting.

Livestock roam the forests in many parts of southern Chile, impacting ground cover, shrubs and saplings, damaging soils and polluting streams, all of which contribute to the demise of forest-dependent wildlife species, including the huemul. Perhaps only 1,000 of these robust creatures remain. Most are in the Aisén Region of southern Chile.

doubled from 6,663 in 1980 to more than 13,000 in 1989.[93]

Information is generally lacking with regard to the genetic diversity of native trees. A major exception is the *Nothofagus* or southern beech genus. The variety and distribution of all ten species are reasonably well understood.[94] Two southern beech trees, raulí and roble, have been examined at length by scientists from CONAF, several universities and the forest industry. In Valdivia, a raulí seed orchard of 20 hectares was established in 1990 for reforestation purposes, and will offer an opportunity to carry out limited genetic research.[95] As with endangered wildlife species, CONAF has invested some effort in the protection of morphological and genetic variability for what may be Chile's three most endangered trees: ruil *(N. alessandri)*, belloto del sur *(Beilschmiedia berteroana)* and queule *(Gomortega keule)*.[96]

In the 1990s, as research expands, a much better picture of genetic diversity in Chilean forests will emerge, particularly for species whose populations have been significantly reduced below desirable levels. Wild plant species that show promise as future sources of domestic crops, medicines or raw materials will likely receive more attention by scientists. New protected areas may also be established containing populations not yet represented in the National System of Protected Wildlands.

A truckload of alerce makes its way out of the Pata Mai region southeast of Puerto Montt. Only dead wood can lawfully be removed from the forest.

❀ Ken Wilcox

Endangered, Vulnerable & Rare Birds
of Chilean Forests

Endangered

Coscoroba swan *(Coscoroba coscoroba)*
Peregrine falcon *(Falco peregrinus anatum)*
Chilean burrowing parrot *(Cyanoliseus patagonius byroni)*

Ruddy-headed goose *(Chloephaga rubidiceps)*
South American pointed snipe
   (Nycticryphes semicollaris)

Vulnerable

Pink-footed shearwater *(Puffinus creatopus)*
Humboldt's penguin *(Spheniscus humboldti)*
Black-faced ibis *(Theristicus caudatus)*
Black-necked swan *(Cygnus melancoryphus)*
Andean condor *(Vultur gryphus)*
South American snipe *(Gallinago gallinago)*
Inca tern *(Larosterna inca)*
Slender-billed parakeet *(Enicognathus leptorhynchus)*
Magellanic woodpecker *(Campephilus magellanicus)*

Peruvian diving petrel *(Pelecanoides garnotii)*
Guaynay cormorant
   (Phalacrocorax bougainvillii)
Andean goose *(Chloephaga melanoptera)*
Osprey *(Pandion haliaetus)*
Grey gull *(Larus modestus)*
Chilean pigeon *(Columba araucana)*
Chilean woodstar *(Eulidia yarrellii)*

Rare

White-necked heron *(Ardea cocoi)*
White-cheeked pintail *(Anas bahamensis)*
Bicolored hawk *(Accipiter bicolor)*
White-throated hawk *(Buteo albigula)*
Gay's seedsnipe *(Attagis gayi)*

Stripe-backed bittern *(Ixobrychus involucris)*
Black-headed duck *(Heteronetta atricapilla)*
Rufous-tailed hawk *(Buteo ventralis)*
Magellanic plover *(Pluvianellus socialis)*
Andean gull *(Larus serranus)*

Note: *Waterfowl and other avian species that utilize open land and water areas adjacent to forests are included.*

Source: CONAF, 1989

Forest Soils

In the largest stand of coastal Chilean rainforest and the smallest microhabitat tucked under a leaf, soils represent the dissolved wreckage of flora and fauna, mountains and bedrock, water, atmosphere and the ages. Healthy soils held together by vegetation are essential to preventing erosion and to maintaining diversity of all forests.

Beneath the trees (and sometimes in the trees) a variety of soils ranging from mineral to organic, wet to dry, acid to alkaline, contribute to an almost infinite variety of living conditions for the largest and tiniest organisms. Soil structure, mineral and moisture content, biological activity and nutrient cycling help determine what can survive and reproduce.

While temperate forest soils are often acidic, neutral and even alkaline soils in central Chile's shrublands can support as many as 108 species on one-tenth of a hectare. Volcanic soils are common in the Chilean Andes—much of it put there by the more than 2,000 volcanoes and cinder cones that exist today, at least 50 of which are active. Intense volcano and earthquake activity exerts a major influence on soils and therefore floral diversity.

Araucaria forests are limited almost exclusively to volcanic soils, and dense stands can be found within sight of many still-active vents.

Outside the Andes, similar plants and animals can be found in volcanic and non-volcanic soils and sediments, yet the ecosystems and habitats that have developed can be quite distinct. A community of shade-tolerant trees, for example, that dominates a climax rainforest in the non-volcanic coastal ranges may be very different from trees growing in a comparable setting in the Andes. Identical plant species can assume different forms from one site to another as well, partially due to soil characteristics.

Soil erosion has become a major concern in Chile as a result of land-clearing, development, over-grazing and tree plantations. The effects that these kinds of intensive activities have on erosion, soil loss, soil organisms, nutrient cycling, water quality and biodiversity are serious and often debated. With the release of a report in 1993, CONAF referred to the problem as "soil cancer," noting that almost half the land area of the nation, or about 35 million hectares, are afflicted.

With leaves that reach eight feet across, the giant nalca (Gunnera chilensis) *is the world's largest herbaceous plant. Nalca is common in Chile's temperate rainforest.*
❀ Peter McBride

3.3 Threatened Ecosystems

Oᴏ OF THE 54 FLORISTIC FORMATIONS REPRESENTED in the National System of Protected Wildlands, only a minority are considered strong representations. The best-protected ecosystems tend to occur in the far south, where 17 out of every 20 hectares in the system are located. Thus, most of Chile's ecosystems are not well protected; all but a few are potentially threatened.

Throughout the country, human impacts to the environment have largely contributed to the listing of more than 200 plant and animal species as rare, vulnerable or endangered. Many others have declined in numbers as a result of direct exploitation: harvesting ruil trees, for example, or hunting pudu or shooting sea-going river otters for fish bait. The introduction of aggressive non-native species that out-compete (or consume) Chilean species in their native habitat is a serious problem as well. Mink introduced into the wild have eradicated native rodent populations in some areas, while Himalayan blackberry has displaced native bird habitat.

In the past, land-clearing for farms and careless or unnecessary burning were the principal causes of deforestation and widespread environmental disruption—a phenomenon that was by no means limited to Chile. With increasing populations, advancing technologies and soaring human appetites for forest resources, the process of environmental degradation has accelerated.

The link between environmental degradation and the classified status of sensitive species is clear. Ruined habitats are not conducive to maintaining healthy populations of native species. In fact, endangered plants and animals are more frequently being recognized as indicator species that reflect the overall health or disarray of ecosystems. Human activities that degrade the environment—fuelwood collection, urbanization, industrial development, plantation forestry—can only contribute to the destruction or displacement of native species. Activities that protect or restore ecosystems can only benefit species. Thus, there is a growing movement in the world to identify and

"It is not an entirely unjustified exaggeration to assert that Chilean forestry is approaching a Monterey pine monoculture, and it is precisely this monoculture which alarms foresters... The future of Chilean forestry would be more secure if Monterey pine were part of a balanced and diverse forestry program which had more flexibility to respond to changing ecologic and economic conditions."

—John Krebs,
Climate: Monterey Pine
[1976][98]

The World's Oldest Trees

Within Chile's forests are some of the oldest known trees in the world. Ancient, or late-successional, forests of the south are comprised of several species that live for hundreds of years and grow to more than a meter across. A handful live to a thousand years and achieve diameters of two meters or more. At least two—alerce and araucaria—exceed two thousand years.

The oldest known tree on Earth is a 4,900-year-old bristlecone pine in the White Mountains of California. Until 1990, the second-oldest tree was also thought to occur in California: a giant sequoia 3,200 years old. But a large alerce stump examined by scientists in 1992 confirmed the tree had lived for more than 3,600 years.[97] Alerces over four meters in diameter are known and a 4,000-year-old tree is not out of the question.

In every sense of the word, ancient Chilean forests are magnificent.

Upper left: alerce (**Fitzroya cupressoides**), *exceeds 3,600 years.*
Upper right: araucaria (**Araucaria araucana**), *exceeds 2,000 years.*
Lower left: bristlecone pine (**Pinus aristata**), *exceeds 4,900 years.*
Lower right: giant sequoia (**Sequoiadendron giganteum**), *exceeds 3,300 years.*
The top two are native to Chile; the bottom two reside in California.
❀ Ken Wilcox, Kim Sallaway (giant sequoia)

safeguard endangered or sensitive ecosystems, not just individual species of concern.

Perhaps the greatest threat to native forest ecosystems is outright clearing, either through burning or clearcut logging practices. Selective cutting can be nearly as disastrous if the best timber (and genetic stock) is removed or soils are made susceptible to erosion. Firewood collection and the introduction of livestock into the forest are major threats as well. Even where reforestation occurs, planting native species is the exception in Chile rather than the rule. Where trees are planted they stand a very good chance of being Monterey pine *(Pinus radiata)*, the exotic wonder tree that is now more widespread in Chile than in any other country in the world.[99]

Mining activities also impact forests, as do ground and surface water withdrawals, human-caused forest fires and environmental contamination. Chile's mining code allows prospecting and mineral exploitation within national parks and other protected areas. The potential for harm is obvious.

Establishing new protected areas (and effective management policies) is one approach to reducing these threats. However, there is no assurance that granting protected status to an area of forest will prevent degradation to large adjoining ecosystems. No matter how successful preservation efforts are over the near-term, millions of hectares of native forest will remain outside the National System of Protected Wildlands. Therefore, policies of good stewardship, conservation and enlightened resource management are essential regardless of the land's protected status. An extra measure of care is warranted where sensitive species or ecosystems are concerned.

While most sensitive species are fairly well recognized as either endangered, vulnerable to extinction or rare, no such characterization exists for ecosystems. Forests that have been heavily exploited are presumed to be in some danger when their range is reduced below what a consensus of experts might consider reasonably sustainable. Such consensus, however, is difficult to achieve. We simply do not know enough about forest ecosystems to be certain how much protected forest is enough.

It is even questionable whether an ecologically based minimum area for any forest exists at all. Any number of calamities such as fire, disease, climate change or ozone depletion could stress, destroy or transform even the largest forest. Perhaps the best we could do is protect all that remains and work toward restoring some of what has been lost. Politically, that may be unrealistic. At the least, we can work toward diminishing the threats from development and exploitation, focus on priorities for preservation and think more realistically about what can be accomplished. That is precisely what is taking place in Chile.

In 1541, trees outnumbered buildings in the sprawling capital city of Santiago. In 1993, CONAF kicked off an ambitious tree-planting project to help improve air quality in the city — one of the world's most polluted. The effort involves planting a million and a half native trees in and around Santiago. The hope is that as the trees mature they will absorb carbon dioxide and replenish oxygen to help counter the frequent inversions that keep the city mired in stagnant air for weeks at a time.
❈ Ken Wilcox

CODEFF, for example, is working on several fronts to protect native forests, from advocating sustainable forestry and challenging attempts by industry to convert native forests to plantations, to supporting indigenous people in their efforts to secure their homeland. The newly established Lahuen Foundation has made forest preservation its top priority and is already a principal player in setting up reserves at the Cañi near Pucón and on Magdalena Island north of Aisén.

Others, including a number of private individuals and foundations both in and outside the country, are investing their own resources into protecting biomass and biodiversity in Chile's native forests. In 1991, the financial pages of Santiago newspapers reported the government's approval of a $7 million private investment in native forest preservation — the first of its kind. At the same time, the Weeden Foundation of New York, Patagonia, Inc. and Esprit-Chile each contributed major shares toward the Cañi acquisition on behalf of Fundación Lahuen and Ancient Forest International with the assistance of the World Parks Endowment Fund.

To focus specifically on needs for preservation throughout Chile, several conferences have been organized including a major biodiversity conference in Santiago. Chilean and international experts are convening to discuss priorities for the protection of ecosystems and the preservation of biodiversity — an appropriate follow-up to the 1992 Earth Summit in Rio de Janeiro. These events bring together the best information currently available on the state of the nation's most sensitive species and ecosystems as well as provide a forum for exchanging ideas on how to best achieve conservation objectives. Ancient Forest International will continue to report on the results of these efforts as they unfold.

A number of critical sites have been identified by Chilean experts that provide opportunities to protect threatened native forest ecosystems (many of these are listed in the next section). Among them are sites in the Maule and Bío-Bío Regions (VII and VIII), where *Nothofagus* forests have largely been replaced by plantations of Monterey pine and eucalyptus. The four most endangered trees in Chile, ruil, pitao, southern belloto and queule, exist here. Three are present in a tiny 45-hectare reserve established at Los Ruiles.[100] On that basis alone, these species can hardly be considered protected. This deficiency of protected areas seriously threatens genetic variability for all four species. A meager total of 794 hectares is currently protected in the Maule Region—the worst statistic for all of Chile.

Farther south, portions of the Valdivian Rainforest, especially within the coastal range, are also listed as high priority sites. As discussed earlier, the floral diversity of many remote areas of the southern coastal cordillera is not well understood. Relict forests like the ancient alerce groves in the Andes and the coast mountains have already generated tremendous interest. Although some alerce stands are slowly regenerating, young trees are conspicuously absent from areas where mature trees are known to reach four meters in diameter and 3,600 years of age.[101] Massive cutting and burning of alerce over the last century reduced these forests to mere fragments of what they once were. What remains are some the world's most magnificent groves, any of which could easily be destroyed. Once lost, the ancient alerce forest can never be reestablished.

Many coastal forest ecosystems, several of which are unprotected, are also of concern, as well as adjacent near-shore marine ecosystems. Microhabitats throughout the country are home to unusual plant communities unmatched anywhere in the world. And considering the high degree of endemism present in these and other environments, the list of critical sites could expand substantially. Botanists, ecologists, forestry agencies and institutions, environmental activists and interested citizens each have their own lists of priorities. Preservation, as noted earlier, is not the only strategy for reducing the threats to native forests.

Apart from outright designation of new protected areas, threatened ecosystems may be safeguarded by decreasing or diffusing the dangers. For example, the forest industry is anxious to convert large areas of native forest to single-species plantations, especially in Regions VI through X. Tree growth rates are most favorable here, and plantations can be established in close proximity to processing facilities and shipping ports. Public policies are needed that conserve native forest biodiversity by preventing or controlling conversion to exotic plantations. In

From the extreme north to the extreme south, dozens of major rivers cut through the Andes, making Chile one of the most spectacular coastal-mountain environments on the planet.
❀ Ken Wilcox

some areas, this approach could, perhaps, be more effective than a strategy of strict preservation if the objective is protecting the long-term viability of certain native forest ecosystems. *Conservation*, as opposed to *preservation*, is integral to the notion of sustainable use of natural resources. Combining these strategies with restoration and enhancement initiatives will accomplish a great deal. Nevertheless, where sensitive species are concerned, outright preservation may be the only workable alternative.

Part 4

Future Forests

OVER THE PAST FIVE CENTURIES, at least half of all native forests have disappeared from the Chilean landscape. Of what remains, only a small amount is undisturbed primary forest. These last remnants account for as little as ten percent of the area of Chile that was forested prior to colonization by Spain. Most of the loss occurred in the wake of European and Chilean settlement across south central Chile and the Valdivian Rainforest region in the second half of the nineteenth century. Widespread cutting and burning accelerated well into the 1900s, consuming the bulk of the nation's oldest trees in a matter of decades.

This fateful process of forest degradation in Chile—and globally as well—may seem to have unfolded very slowly. Yet one can gaze into the shallow crown of a young araucaria tree and imagine all the destruction that has taken place during the lifetime of that tree. On the timetable of a 3,000-year-old alerce, the trend is ominous.

What might become of the remaining stands of primary forest over the next five centuries? The next 150 years? Will half again disappear? Will the world's increasing population, demand for wood and paper products, ever-consuming behavior and technologies, and the struggle for economic development bring unbearable stress to all that is left of native forest ecosystems? Or will humanity work to protect and restore the integrity and diversity of wild forests before much more is lost? Even if humanity is able to end the destruction of forests today, what do climate change, atmospheric ozone depletion and the steady loss of biodiversity promise for future forests?

How can we guarantee a sufficient level of conservation of all existing forest types? How can we manage remaining forests in ways that guarantee the future viability of every Chilean plant or animal species? Is it enough to guard against all further cutting in the most ancient of Chilean forests, the alerce and araucaria, so

Coihue and alerce often mingle in the higher elevations of the Valdivian Rainforest.
❀ Ken Wilcox

they might persist through the next millennium? Or has too much damage already been done?

To answer these questions, we must continually educate ourselves and identify priorities for preservation as best we can. Concerned Chileans and those of us in the global community who fully respect their efforts can focus on forest ecosystems that make the most sense to protect now and those areas which could be managed for resource production on an ecologically sustainable basis. We can examine which areas can be restored.

We can change the way we perceive the landscape as a whole and acknowledge that when we utilize any part of it for some economic advantage, it is often at the expense of species and natural communities. This is not to say that we cannot exploit the natural environment for our own good — as every other living species does — but we do need to be aware of the consequences of our actions. Forest resources can be put to good use without destroying forests. In Chile, for example, sustainable forestry and ecotourism can become model industries if developed in ecologically, culturally and economically sensible ways.

With the level of commitment to the environment already apparent in Chile today, real solutions to these issues are not far off. According to many Chilean forest experts, there is still time to act.

In the following pages, we address a few of the questions that leading Chilean ecologists and activists are grappling with in the 1990s. The issues and priorities presented here are widely recognized and debated by many who are concerned about the welfare of Chileans as well as the future well-being of the nation's native forest heritage.

Magellanic woodpecker (Campephilus magellanicus), *also known as carpintero negro, is Chile's largest woodpecker. This forest-dependent bird has suffered from habitat loss and is listed as vulnerable to extinction.*
❀ Peter McBride

4.1 Securing Biodiversity in Chile

By Adriana Hoffmann
Defenders of the Chilean Forest, Lahuen Foundation

THE PRESERVATION OF CHILE'S NATURAL HERITAGE constitutes an inevitable responsibility for our generation. This is the reason why around a hundred specialists on this subject got together to define the most important areas where biodiversity is concentrated in our country, so as to protect them from man's actions.

Approximately 100 academic "preservationists" and administrators of Chile's national heritage were called together by CONAF in early 1993. They came from all over the country and met during three days in Santiago, with the purpose of defining and selecting the most important areas where biodiversity is represented in our country, so it can be completely included in the National System of Protected Wildlands.

The Criteria

Different points of view, both ecological and practical, were considered to define the more important areas. The most outstanding points were:

- *The representativeness and exclusiveness of the ecosystems proposed;*
- *Diverse habitats and associations represented in the chosen areas;*
- *Valuable species and endemism;*
- *Pristine aspects of the lower level of perturbation in the area;*
- *That the places are large enough to allow the conservation of vital processes for the organisms living in the ecosystem.*

Among the practical points of view, susceptibility to degradation due to man's actions (places threatened by being disturbed) and value for research or monitoring were main considerations.

However, something became clear: the general lack of basic

knowledge about Chilean biota in most parts of the country and within most of the different groups of organisms. It seems that there exists relatively complete scientific knowledge concerning only the terrestrial vascular plants, terrestrial vertebrates, and some other small groups. If we consider that there are approximately 34,000 organisms described by science in Chile, it is thought that at least the same number of unknown species exist.

There is little knowledge concerning the biology, geographic distribution, and ecological interconnections between the organisms and their environment. What everybody did learn very well during the meeting was that there is a lot more to be learned.

The Places

A group of experts from the University of Concepcion prepared a proposal to be discussed during the symposium named "Priority Areas for the Conservation of the Biological Diversity in Chile." Having these documents as a base, there were three subcommittees formed to study in detail and accept, modify, or propose new areas to fulfill the objective of preserving, in the best way possible, the richness of the plants, animals, and fungi that constitute biodiversity in the Chilean landscape.

During the first stage of this initiative the assembly worked on terrestrial ecosystems, but always considering the importance of protecting marine ecosystems and the close interaction that exists among all of the systems.

The job of locating, evaluating and prioritizing 72 sites throughout Chile was an extraordinarily rich experience (*the list of priority sites begins on p. 110*). Astonishing and surprising was the knowledge and the love that so many people feel for nature and all its countless expressions.

Also, a long list of small areas was proposed in which the conservation of species is very important where both plants and animals are endangered, vulnerable, or rare. Also analyzed, was the possibility of protecting areas of biodiversity concentration in the Chilean Antarctic territory.

The job done by the symposium of identifying the places that are left in Chile with well represented biodiversity is a unique initiative in Latin America. Now, it all depends on the authorities to approve these suggestions and to contribute the necessary budget to implement and oversee a complete National System of Protected Wildlands.

We must all support this valuable effort.   *A.H.*

← *Coihue, Chile's largest broadleaf tree.*   ❀ Adriana Hoffmann

4.2 Native Forest Priorities

THE ISSUE OF TEMPERATE FOREST CONSERVATION is not limited to Chile but is one that is being addressed throughout the world's temperate latitudes. Enduring protection for all ancient forest ecosystems has been and will continue to be a high priority in many countries both north and south of the equator. People in Chile—foresters, scientists, ecologists, community leaders, public officials and concerned citizens alike—are working diligently to analyze the current threats to native forest ecosystems and biodiversity, to identify opportunities for the development of sustainable forestry, and to determine specific priorities for preservation.

The following list of land preservation and forest conservation needs and priorities emerged from an exhaustive literature search and countless interviews and forums conducted in Chile since 1989, including a March 1993 Santiago conference hosted by CONAF which identified and set priorities for conservation objectives in Chile. The list identifies a variety of needs and priorities as expressed by concerned Chileans, including:

- *Land preservation priorities*
- *Resource conservation needs*
- *Scientific research needs*
- *Public policy needs*

Preservation priorities begin with a few general recommendations followed by a listing of specific sites that have been recommended by Chilean experts to CONAF for inclusion in the National System of Protected Wildlands.[102] Sites range from "most urgent" and "very important" to those of "significant interest." The recommendations also include non-forested areas and are current as of 1993. Modifications can be expected as circumstances change and new information becomes available.

Land Preservation Priorities

- Establish new additions to the National System of Protected Wildlands that contain viable representations of currently unprotected native forest ecosystems.
- Enlarge or supplement those protected areas containing ecosystems that are poorly represented.
- Acquire new protected areas in central Chile (all Regions) that provide suitable habitat for rare, vulnerable or endangered species of plants and animals.
- Ensure an equitable distribution of protected areas throughout the forested regions of the country so that all Chileans, now and in the future, have the opportunity to experience them and share in their stewardship. (The central regions of the country require special attention.)
- Designate large areas of undisturbed *siempreverde* (evergreen) forest for preservation within the Valdivian Rainforest of Region X, particularly in the Coastal Range.
- Establish protected area boundaries based on ecological parameters rather than political ones; and actively support the designation of world biosphere reserves, world parks and similar sites that recognize and protect the integrity of greater ecosystems and landscapes.
- Designate degraded forests and select unforested lands for sustainable forestry projects in all forest regions.

Areas recommended to CONAF in 1993 for inclusion in the National System of Protected Wildlands begin on the next page.

"It is very important... to buy lands for [both] preservation and the application of conservation silviculture...."

—Claudio Donoso,
University Austral
Valdivia

Chile's temperate rainforest supports one of the highest concentrations of biomass of any forest in the world.
❀ Ken Wilcox

Most Urgent

- Extend Lauca National Park limits and Las Vicuñas National Reserve toward the lowest areas, to the elevation of 1500 meters above sea level, including Cerro Chapiquiña.
- Coposa and Huasco Salars in the Tarapacá Region, Iquique Mountain Range.
- Mejillones Peninsula, including Cerro Moreno and the bordering islands, Antofagasta Coast.
- Paposo, the entire coastal area from the El Cobre fishing community south to Pan de Azúcar National Park, Taltal Coast.
- Negro Francisco and Santa Rosa lagoons, and the lower reaches of the high Andean region east of Copiapó.
- Challe and Carrizal Bajo plain areas, along the coast from Huasco north to Totoral, in the Atacama Region (*National Park, 1994*).
- Teatinos Point up to Quebrada Honda, including the small islands named Pajaros on the coast north of La Serena.
- Yali Estuary and King's Lagoon, on the Santiago Coast south of Santo Domingo.
- The Cantillana Highlands and Aculeo Lagoon, south of Santiago.
- Radal Siete Tazas and the bordering area of the Claro River, in the Molina Mountain Range.
- Vilches Highlands in the foothills of the mountain range in Talca.
- Hormillos and the valley of Ancoa River in the Linares Mountain Range.
- The Maule Oaks, including Los Ruiles National Reserve, near Cauquenes in the Maule Region.
- Tregualemu and Ramadillas, in the mountain range along the coast of the Maule Region.
- Bullileo and Suárez Lagoon, in the foothills of the Andes between Parral and San Carlos.
- Cerro Cayumanqui, north of Concepcion, between the Itata and Andalien Rivers.
- The snow mountains in Chillán, including Shangri-La and Termas de Chillán, and El Purgatorio in the Andes of the Bío-Bío Region.
- Extension of Nahuelbuta National Park northeast to Caramávida.
- Raulí forests in the Pirehueico, Panguipulli, Choshuenco region south of Villarica.
- Pelada Mountain Range: coastal mountains south of Corral, between the Contaco and Bueno Rivers, from La Unión to Osorno.

Darwin's frog (Rhinoderma darwini) *is another forest-dependent species listed as vulnerable to extinction. A similar frog* (R. rufum) *is endangered.*
❀ Peter McBride

Very Important

- Licancábur-Tatio Geisers in the high valley of the Loa River, Antofagasta (*National Park, 1995*).
- Llullaillaco, including the Frío River and Punta Negra Salar, also in Antofagasta (*National Park, 1995*).
- The deep valley of the Valeria River, including Valeria Lagoons, Chica and Grande, in the high Andes east of Vallenar.
- Illapel Mountain Range areas.
- Santa Ines (Pichidangui) and Cerros Los Molles, on the coast along the border between Coquimbo and Valparaíso Regions.
- "El Tigre" ravine in Zapallar, in the coast mountains north of Valparaíso.
- El Melón slope, in Quillota Province of the Valparaíso Region.
- Humid forests near Quintero and Mantagua, in the coastal region between Concón and Quintero.
- Alicahue, in the foothills of the mountain range in Petorca Province of Region V.
- Extension of La Campana National Park to El Roble, including the upper reaches of the Vizcachas and Chilauna ranges, between the Metropolitan and Valparaíso Regions.
- La Estrella and Cerro Nombre, near Empedrado in the Maule Region.
- Prairies and natural humid lowlands of native species in the Cholchol River, from Imperial to Angol, in Region IX.
- Mana Esthor in the central depression of the Malleco Province, in the Araucania Region.
- Budi Lake, Trovolhue Lagoon and the Imperial River outlet on the coast west of Temuco.
- Cruces River, an area of streams and tributaries near Valdivia, a dune zone in Junguillar.
- Flat lowlands in Mahuidanchi and La Paz in the Lastania slope, in the province of Valdivia.
- Cudico, near La Union, in the Lakes Region.
- Monte Verde, the formation of Ñadis and interesting archeological traces, near Puerto Montt in Region X.
- Guafo Island, off the southwest tip of Chiloé in Region X.
- Extension of Hornopirén National Park including glaciers and native forests of Pata Mai and the valley of Contao River.
- Futalefú, in Palena Province southeast of Chaitén.
- Chacabuco River Valley, in Aisén Province.
- Lomas Bay on the Strait of Magellan, Tierra del Fuego.
- The south-central area of Tierra del Fuego Island, between Vicuña-Cameron and Almirantazgo Fiord, in Region XII.
- Diego Ramirez Islands, at the south end of the Tierra del Fuego and Cape Horn, the southern extreme of the national territory.

"We could never hope to adequately protect biological diversity solely through preservation...."

—Jerry Franklin
University of Washington
Seattle

Significant Interest

Puma tracks in the snow near Quinquen, at the head-waters of the Bío-Bío River.
❀ Ken Wilcox

- Cerro Camaraca and Vitor Ravine on the coast of Region I.
- Yuta and Azapa Ravines and the outlet of the Camarones Ravine, in the Tarapacá Region.
- Extension of Los Flamencos National Reserve to the Captive Salars in the Andes east of Antofagasta.
- Obispito, Flamenco and Los Leones Ravines, near Chañaral, on the coast of the Atacama Region.
- The Green Lagoon in the Copiapó Mountains.
- The lowlands of Travesia and Pajaritos to protect the flavery desert at the south of Copiapó.
- Las Juntas on the Copiapó River.
- The Desuenturadas Islands: San Felipe and San Antonio.
- Pajonales slope, between La Serena and Vallenar, in the Atacama Region.
- Condoriaco, in the coastal mountains north of the La Serena.
- Huanta and Banos del Toro, in the Doña Ana mountains, east of La Serena.
- El Nague and Palo Colorado, in the Coquimbo Region.
- Lengua de Vaca Point, near Tongoy in the Coquimbo Region.
- Mialgui, just east of Ovalle-Monte Patria, in Region IV.
- Tabaco Hill, in Region V.
- Cordoba Ravine, in El Tabo, in the Valparaíso Region.
- Tilama-Pedegua, Fifth Region.
- Huenchun Ranch, in the Metropolitan Region.
- Marshy area at Batuco, Metropolitan Region.
- El Volcán, in Cajon del Maipo, Metropolitan Region.
- Barros Negros and El Manzano ravines near Farellones, in the Santiago Andes, Metropolitan Region.
- Los Alpes on the Clarillo River, southeast of San Fernando, in Region VI.
- The hills of Eswadron, south of Talcahuano, in the Bío-Bío Region.
- The Archipielago of Huiqripilan, south of Chiloé.
- Aycará, on Huequi Peninsula, Palena Province in Region X.
- Add Contramaestre Island to Los Pinguinos Natural Monument on the Strait of Magellan.

Resource Conservation Needs

- Conserve biological diversity at all levels, including ecosystems, species and gene pools.
- Maintain viable populations of all endemic species: safeguard sufficient habitat, control exploitation of sensitive species, and discourage the introduction of non-native species.

- Develop and implement sustainable forestry alternatives to large-scale clearing and replanting with exotic species; projects should be designed to sustain both economic and environmental values over the long term.
- Engage in the restoration of degraded forests.
- In all regions, establish managed woodlots with fast-growing tree species (native or exotic) for the production of fuelwood.
- Safeguard water quality and conserve soils in all forested watersheds through the use of appropriate harvest techniques and land use development activities.
- Provide unobstructed wildlife corridors that interconnect principal habitat areas.

Scientific Research Needs

- Map and evaluate the National System of Protected Wildlands and other public or private programs for land preservation to establish a complete inventory of native forest ecosystems that are adequately protected, poorly protected and unprotected.
- Determine land acquisition priorities for ecosystems that are poorly protected or unprotected.
- Generate funding to support Chilean research efforts in biodiversity, forest ecology, the population and distribution of species, forest conservation, conservation biology, ecosystem restoration and sustainable development.
- Expand existing academic programs and facilities that serve the study and conservation of native forests.
- Support international efforts to understand the implications of global climate change and ozone depletion for temperate forests in the southern hemisphere.

Public Policy Needs

- Institute national policies for sustainable forestry and ecosystem-based management of all forest resources.
- Ensure adequate enforcement of management plans and regulations; respond quickly and decisively to violations.
- Curtail clearcut logging methods and intentional burning as a means of clearing land or harvesting forest resources.
- Disallow reforestation subsidies that result in the conversion of native forests (regardless of their condition) to exotic-species plantations.
- Encourage wood chip production and fuel wood collection in degraded native forests only in concert with a comprehensive program for restoration.

Chileans Caring for the Environment

Chileans, as a society, are strong advocates for a healthy environment. A Gallop poll conducted in 1992 found that 74% of Chilean women and 66% of Chilean men feel that protecting the environment is more important than economic development. Two-thirds feel that the environment is in bad shape, and nearly four out of five hold Chilean and foreign companies equally responsible. A majority said they were willing to buy "green" products if given the opportunity.[103]

An industry-sponsored poll conducted in 1992 found that a large majority of people are opposed destroying native forests or replacing them with exotic plantations. Most felt that the total area of forests had decreased over the previous 20 years due primarily to indiscriminate exploitation and secondarily to fire and development.[104]

In the winter of 1993, a

[Continued on p. 114]

[continued from p. 113]

large group of young people carrying native tree saplings delivered 60,000 signatures to President Aylwin in support of native forest conservation.

The Aylwin government helped to establish a comprehensive national environmental policy through legislation that coordinates the actions of agencies and institutions, develops a variety of new programs and policies, and provides for environmental impact assessment of major projects. The World Bank has provided loans to assist in these endeavors as well as to promote education and technical training, and to help fund a nationwide inventory of native forests—the first in thirty years.

The forest inventory includes satellite imagery that will give CONAF the ability to track illegal logging operations as well. CODEFF has conducted its own aerial reconnaissance of native forests in southern Chile and has discovered widespread problems with illegal cutting.[105] Public concern has helped bring about better enforcement and stiffer penalties against violators.

- Encourage the use of mixed native species in place of exotic plantations on cutover or non-forested lands; promote tree-planting by all Chileans as a responsible means of reforesting the Earth.
- Discourage or prohibit the use of plantation seedling "kits" or similar practices where they might induce the random conversion of native forests to exotic plantations.
- Diversify local economies to avoid excessive dependence on forest resources.
- Develop international markets for sustainable forestry products derived from native species.
- Improve public environmental education programs, with a strong emphasis on forest conservation, land stewardship and interpretive programs.
- Discourage uncontrolled livestock grazing within recovering or relatively undisturbed native forests.
- Enhance management of national parks and other wildlands, particularly with respect to water rights, mineral exploration, timber poaching, livestock grazing, tourism development, off-road vehicle use, hydropower development, and protection of archaeological resources.
- Protect water quality through the prevention of soil erosion and by discouraging the application of pesticides.
- Encourage and facilitate paper recycling and wood fiber conservation in all urban areas.

Ancient Coihue tree at timberline, Valdivian Rainforest. ❀ Ken Wilcox

4.3 Sustainable Forestry Opportunities

Sustainable forestry, like sustainable development generally, is an approach to forestry that provides a means of satisfying people's needs for wood products today without compromising the forest ecosystem or the capacity of future generations to satisfy their needs.[106] Sustainability implies a non-destructive relationship with native forest ecosystems. The object of sustainable forestry is simple: to use forest resources for the good of society without destroying the forest. To some, sustainable forestry seems to be a contradiction in terms. Is it possible to harvest resources and protect the forest simultaneously? The answer, of course, is yes. Some people have been doing it for centuries.

While many indigenous cultures, like the Pehuenche people living among the araucaria forests in south-central Chile, have practiced sustainable forestry for countless generations, Western industrialized societies have just begun to define what is really a very old concept. The simple elegance of taking only what you need tempered by a sense of reverence for nature's gifts is at the heart of both ancient and contemporary notions of sustainable forestry. However, we live in an era of powerful and complex economies, in an international marketplace where levels of consumption and waste are unprecedented, and where the demands for forest resources are enormous. Against stiff corporate competition, producers are reluctant to temper their investments with "reverence."

With that in mind, can sustainable forestry measure up to both economic and environmental challenges? In Chile the prospects are at least promising.

Governments and citizens worldwide have begun to recognize the effects that our numbers, our technologies and our appetites for forest products have had on native forests. We are becoming much more sensitive to the long-term social, economic and ecological benefits of protecting natural forests. And we are learning that we can no longer take them for granted. Problems

"Stemming the erosion of life on earth will require not only protecting nature reserves and indigenous homelands, but integrating the protection of diversity into the "mainstream" patterns of production, consumption, and waste disposal as well. In short, the conservation of bio-diversity should guide all economic development."[107]

—John C. Ryan,
Worldwatch Paper #108,
"Life Support: Conserving
Biological Diversity"
[1992]

This young alerce tree will require at least a thousand years to reach the size of its neighbors in the background, yet even the noble alerce has something to offer sustainable forestry. Dead wood collected by alerceros contributes a high-quality resource to local communities. If the wood was collected on a large-scale commercial basis it would be quickly depleted and an economic niche that serves a significant number of people would be lost.
❀ Steve Gilroy

"When we talk about sustainable development, we are thinking about economic growth with social equity and care of our natural resources."[108]

—Patricio Aylwin,
President of Chile, 1990-94
Rio Earth Summit, 1992

of deforestation, degradation, soil erosion, habitat loss, and a host of adverse environmental effects only emphasize the need for change in the way we manage native forests. Yet, the shift away from conventional industrial forestry, clearcut logging practices, and indiscriminate cutting and burning of forests for agriculture and fuelwood will not occur overnight.

In Chile and elsewhere, visionary public policies must be debated and adopted and new technologies developed to minimize the impacts of exploitation and to optimize the use and conservation of wood products. (The public policy debate in Chile began in earnest prior to publication of this report. Comprehensive native forest legislation was introduced in Congress by the Aylwin government in April 1992 and by late 1995 the new law had yet to be adopted; the outcome cannot be predicted.) Alternative energies and efficient technologies for wood-based cooking and heating need to be made available to large segments of the population. Paper recycling programs, already a successful enterprise providing thousands of jobs in Chile, could be expanded. Non-timber forest products such as seeds, leaves, dyes, fruits and medicines need to be protected and markets oriented to sustainability.

Before these changes can be instituted, much more needs to be learned about the composition of native forests and how they function as ecosystems. As a global society we need to nurture a deeper understanding of the ecology of the forest in practical, scientific and spiritual terms. In Chile, substantial information is seriously lacking for most forest types, particularly in Region X, where half the nation's productive native forest occurs. Model projects in sustainable forestry are needed to generate additional data for practical applications and to demonstrate viable alternatives to people in local communities. There are strong indications that more progress may soon be made in Chile in both ecosystem research and sustainable forestry development.

For example, Chile is among 86 developing nations participating in a Forestry Action Plan sponsored by the United Nations and the World Bank, which offers technical and financial support for the development of sustainable forestry projects.[109] Holland has already contributed close to US$1 million to the Chilean effort.[110] In a separate initiative, Italy promised another $1 million (in 1992) to go toward preparation of a comprehensive program for sustainable development on the island of Chiloé in Region X. Forestry will be an important element of that program.[111]

Also in 1992, the U.S., France, Scotland and Italy all contributed to a new $2 million forest research program at the University of Chile. The program is intended to investigate the composition of native forest ecosystems and identify opportunities for sustainable use of native forest resources.[112] The European Economic Community agreed to fund a study of Nothofagus species in southern Chile beginning in 1993, with the hope of finding ways to optimize tree growth which could expand the commercial viability of native species.[113] The U.S. government's *Initiative for the Americas* is projected to divert as much as $39 million in interest payments on Chile's foreign debt to a variety of environmental projects over the next ten years.[114] The Clinton/Gore administration could further the cause if environmental rhetoric solidifies into real action. Sustainable forestry projects are logical candidates for funding. Promising as these developments might appear, industrial investments in conventional forestry far exceed all known investments in sustainable forestry and related research.

Despite the sudden appearance of new research dollars for sustainable forestry, many ecologists are, for several reasons, expressing only cautious optimism. First, the forest industry in Chile is expanding at a frightening pace and the threats to native forests from chipping and conversions to pine plantations will continue to intensify in the foreseeable future. Secondly, much of the data available today with respect to native trees and forest resources dates from the 1960s. New data will be slow in coming. Thus, some experts including biologist Adriana Hoffmann have called for a 10-year moratorium on large-scale cutting in native forests while research proceeds on the composition and extent of native forest ecosystems.[115] Such forward-thinking strategies are similar to those used by New Zealand and Tasmania in the 1980s.

Currently, plantation forestry is the principal source for Chile's record-breaking wood chip and pulp exports. As discussed in Part 2, native forests were not contributing substantial dollars

"You have to start with love for the earth, for nature."

—Miguel Melinir,
Quinquen, 1991

A poster in Chile objects to the destruction of native forests and the export of chips and unprocessed logs.
❀ Ken Wilcox

Sustaining Forests: A Global Priority

As a major policy issue, the cause for sustainable forestry is gaining ground worldwide. On the heels of the Rio Summit in 1992 and the signing by more than 150 countries of the International Convention on Biological Diversity, a new World Commission on Forests and Sustainable Development is being assembled through the United Nations. The Commission's Organizing Committee, chaired by Ambassador Ola Ullsten, former Prime Minister of Sweden, explained the Commission's objectives as follows:

...to advance forest issues as part of the mainstream of economic development. It would marshall the most objective scientific information available on the stage of the world's forests and on the consequences of rapid changes now underway. It would examine land use practices, multiple forest uses, the causes of deforestation and forest degradation, and consider how to reduce the pressures on forests. It would assess the social, economic, political and ecological issues surrounding forests and development and bring in practical proposals for improvement.

Sustainable forestry is also a major theme of interest to IUCN, the World Conservation Union. Established in 1948, IUCN brings together more than 700 public agencies and nongovernmental organizations from 118 countries to accomplish the following:

- *To secure the conservation of nature, and especially of biological diversity, as an essential foundation for the future;*
- *To ensure that where the earth's natural resources are used, this is done in a wise, equitable and sustainable way;*
- *To guide the development of human communities towards ways of life that are both of good quality and in enduring harmony with other components of the biosphere.*

In furtherance of these objectives, IUCN's Forest Conservation Programme strives to conserve forest species and ecological processes, while promoting forest uses which are compatible with the conservation of biological diversity. Field projects are supported and data is collected by the World Conservation Monitoring Centre. IUCN's World Conservation Strategy is served by reconciling conservation and human needs, with a special emphasis on promoting compatible uses around protected areas.

On a more grassroots level, many local, national and international environmental groups are pushing for ecologically sustainable approaches to forestry as well. The Institute for Sustainable Forestry, located in the heart of California's redwood country, advocates for new forestry practices that protect and/or restore natural forest diversity. The Institute is also developing an ecological forest products certification program so consumers will know just what they are purchasing.

Certification is a key to ecoforestry and ensures that a range of issues, from habitat impacts to value-added products, are properly dealt with.

The Ecoforestry Institute (EI), with offices in Oregon State and British Columbia, is "dedicated to natural selection ecoforestry which preserves and restores the complexity and diversity of natural forests." EI is committed to ecologically responsible forestry and supports harvests that rely on "evolutionary natural selection indicators in deciding which trees can be removed from a forest." The concept is based on the assumption that nature knows better than we do how to manage native forest ecosystems.

Ecotrust, affiliated with Conservation International, has also embarked on several sustainable forestry projects in the Pacific Northwest, all of them ambitious and promising in the struggle to rethink our relationship with forest ecosystems.

to the forest-export economy until recently. A moratorium or other restrictions on cutting native forests, therefore, would still not severely disrupt the forestry sector as a whole. To delay increased cutting and further conversions of native forest to exotic plantations in order to study the forest makes sense as a long-term investment in Chile for the benefit of forest resources, the economy and the environment.

CODEFF has suggested that the industry consider reforesting up to 3.5 million hectares of suitable lands that are currently unforested.[116] This is more than double the amount of land already committed to commercial production of pine and eucalyptus. Reforestation projects should focus on mixed stands of native species rather than solely exotic species. However, neither government nor industry have established large-scale nurseries for native tree species, a point that underscores the lack of interest in sustainable forestry on the part of most industrial foresters.

Nevertheless, the establishment of exotic-species plantations is of less concern to environmentalists when there is no loss of native forest involved. CODEFF is also demanding an immediate end to the high-grading of native forests for wood chips and has urged the industry to pursue its role in Chile's development without destroying the nation's natural heritage.

CODEFF has demonstrated its commitment to improving environmental as well as social and economic conditions through a number of initiatives, research projects, publications, and events. These include sponsorship of the nation's first conference on sustainable management of native forests in January 1994 at Austral University in Valdivia which focused on the experiences and knowledge of small-scale foresters.

The problem of *campesinos* clearing forests for fuelwood or to sell timber to chipping plants presents another lofty challenge, and without adequate enforcement, a moratorium could be of dubious efficacy. The industry organization, CORMA, estimated that in the late 1980s the cutting of native forests for fuelwood by the rural population consumed four times as much native wood as the chipping industry.[117] CORMA advocates alternative wood-burning technologies and energy sources as a long-term solution to the problem.

CODEFF has gone a step further by proposing that the government help train small landowners in the sustainable management of native forests and provide grants for their protection and development. A broad program to build public awareness of deforestation globally may help convince people of the need to plant trees in their own backyards.

There is—and will continue to be—much controversy regarding how to best manage native forests on a sustainable

"Tree planting may lack the glory and grandeur of a medical breakthrough, a huge hydropower dam, or any number of technological marvels. But its unmatched potential for stabilizing simultaneously the carbon cycle, land and water resources, rural energy supplies, and people's livelihoods makes it a top priority for economic and social development."

Worldwatch Paper #83,
"Reforesting the Earth"
[1988]

basis. Industry will argue that "over-mature" trees are "going to waste" and ought to be harvested. Ecologists will insist that dying trees are essential to nutrient cycling, forest regeneration and habitat for wildlife. CONAF has argued that sustainable forestry cannot take place on slopes steeper than 30° (50 percent).[118] The industry argues for 45° (100 percent). Chilean society demands that the forests be well-protected, even at the risk of slowing development, according to recent polls.[119] At the same time, individuals and corporations demand autonomy in deciding how to manage their lands for their own best interests.

In the pehuen forest, there are no written laws, no bureaucracy, and little controversy regarding what is best for the forest's future. But there are also very few people and minimal technology with which to exploit the environment. Most of the work is done by hand or with oxen. Resources are carefully looked after as a matter of routine and respect for nature. Only a small percentage of the available piñones (araucaria nuts) are harvested by the Pehuenche people. Some are sprinkled over the roots of trees to help fertilize the soil and ensure a sustainable harvest in coming seasons. The sustainable methods used by the Pehuenche seem almost too easy, not technical enough. Yet, these kinds of models provide good foundations to build sustainability on — even for the high-tech, fast-paced consumer societies of the industrialized world.

Once Chile's native forests are better understood, reforestation projects can be successfully implemented, commercial silviculture and small-scale harvest operations developed, and unique woods processed locally for specialized applications. New compounds for medical use may be discovered, valuable new food products might emerge, export markets could be enhanced for other non-timber forest resources, and low-impact recreation and eco-tourism economies could be developed.

If such efforts are not made, then the debate shifts back to one of preservation versus exploitation. Sustainable forestry, although largely unexplored, offers a kind of middle ground. Sustainable forestry is no substitute for preservation where threatened or scarce ecosystems are concerned, but does offer some promising alternatives in the use and development of Chile's native forests in the coming decades.

For more information on sustainable forestry in Chile, contact CODEFF or CONAF in Santiago, or write to the Institute for Sustainable Forestry, P.O. Box 1580, Redway, CA 95560 USA, or to the Ecoforestry Institute, P. O. Box 5783, Station B, Victoria, B.C. V8R 6S8, Canada.

4.4 Ecotourism: Problems & Potential

IN CHILE, TOURISM IS FAST BECOMING one of the nation's leading growth industries. It is also one of the fastest-growing tourist destinations in the world, according to British sources.[120] Ocean beaches, deserts, spectacular mountains, ski resorts, historic cities, the sprawling capital of Santiago and a host of parks and natural areas offer the most popular destinations.

Nearly a million people, most of them from the U.S., Western Europe and Latin America, visited Chile in 1990.[121] SERNATUR, the National Tourism Service, estimates 1993 tourism revenues at more than $1 billion and a total of 1.4 million visitors, up 96.5 percent over the previous four years. In 1985, tourists spent closer to $60 million. Although neighboring Argentina supplies the largest influx of tourists, travelers from North America and Western Europe are bringing in the bulk of the revenue.

Including Chilean tourists, protected areas accounted for a quarter of a million visitors in 1978 and 600,000 by 1985, despite the fact that CONAF was not actively promoting tourism because of a general lack of facilities and staff. In the same year, only 595 rangers were paid to manage the nation's entire protected wildlands system.[122] Nearly a million people visited protected areas in 1994. The Lakes District (Regions IX and X) accounted for the largest share nationwide with forty percent of all visitors.

The success of tourism in the 1990s means staff support is likely to increase substantially and ongoing improvements will allow more people to enjoy Chile's natural areas without impacting them adversely. With careful planning, tourism development can help protect native forest ecosystems.

Tourism is an enormous industry worldwide that pays the salaries of more than 100 million people, according to the World Travel and Tourism Council.[123] Nature-oriented tourism in all countries attracts tens of billions of dollars each year. What portion of this money makes its way to Chile is uncertain, although many agree that the potential for tourism is great and far from being fully developed—unusual for a country with so many distinct and outstanding natural landscapes.

In 1993, tourism in Chile generated an estimated 200,000 jobs and a total annual income of more than $820 million, an amount equal to 25% of copper exports or 94% of all fruit exports during the same year.[124]

The famed Bío-Bío River which attracts thousands of tourists each year is about to become Chile's greatest loss for ecotourism. With the financial support of the World Bank, a sustainable, income producing, natural environment will give way to the construction of six large dams on the river's wildest reach in order to supply cheap power to industrial growth in south-central Chile. The power barons are also targeting the next best river, the Futalefú, near Chaitén, despite widespread opposition.

❀ Dennis Murphy

To enhance the contribution that tourism makes to national and local economies, the Aylwin government initiated a number of tourism programs and projects around the country, some of them oriented to natural areas. For instance, roads and other access facilities are being improved in the Lakes District so that more visitors can experience the region's superb scenery and recreation opportunities. Some of the more popular parks are being upgraded. The impetus for these efforts is largely economic: the more comfortable and entertained the visitors are, the more likely they will be to make longer or more frequent visits, or to recommend a visit to friends and family. Both public and private sectors have increased their investments considerably in tourism promotion outside the country.

European and North American tourists, principal targets of the industry, have a tendency to seek out beautiful places that are relatively untouched by industrialized society. In fact, CONAF statistics reveal that there are often more Europeans than Chileans visiting the national parks system annually.[125] However, with people comes an assortment of problems and impacts that can actually diminish the quality of the experience they are seeking. The entrepreneurs who accommodate visitors can generate even greater impacts on the environment by way of inadequate facilities (sanitation, water, trails, campsites) or improper or poorly located development such as resorts, hotels and restaurants.

Roads and highways that are improved for tourism can also impact communities and natural areas in unexpected ways. For example, some are calling for an extension of the Carretera Austral, Chile's southern highway, all the way to Puerto Natales in the far south. However, others contend that the highway would open up vast areas of coastal mountains and remote valleys to forest and mineral exploitation, fire, development, and the introduction of alien species into pristine wilderness.

Where environmental goals are concomitant with economic objectives, tourism can play a beneficial role in the protection of wildlands. Where indigenous people depend on the same wildlands for their livelihoods, tourism can be a constructive force in safeguarding valuable resources — assuming, of course, that conflicts between tourists and native people can be avoided.

The notion of environmentally and culturally responsible tourism, or "ecotourism," is receiving a great deal of attention in Chile as it has throughout much of the developing world over the past decade. Those countries with rich, unique, exciting or dramatic landscapes (like Chile) have discovered that people from around the world are eager to visit such places and are willing to spend substantial sums of money for the opportunity. Dollars that hundreds of thousands of visitors spend on airfare,

Ecotourism on Chiloé Island

In 1995, the government returned 4,000 hectares of Chiloé National Park to a Huilliche community of 320 families. The move allows indigenous people who have occupied the area for generations to maintain their traditional way of life while making a beautiful part of the mystical island of Chiloé available for ecotourism.

The southern Andes, though difficult to access, offers an exciting and challenging destination for adventure travelers. This scene is southeast of Puerto Montt near Doug Tompkins' proposed Pumalin Park (see p. 28).
❀ Kim Sallaway

lodging, ground transportation, meals, entertainment and gifts has been called a "pillar of the economy" in the Chilean press.[126]

Interestingly, most visitors to Chile do manage to find their way into the forested regions of the country. One reason for this could be that the natural beauty of the forest is often portrayed in promotional materials and travel guides. Another could be the draw of the forest itself. Non-forested wildlands often occur as desert, tundra or high mountains where climate extremes are much less inviting. Whatever the reason, little information is available regarding the relationship or importance of native forests to tourism. Certainly, large, healthy and mature ecosystems are much more attractive for recreation and scenic enjoyment than cleared, fragmented or degraded forests, or rows and rows of pine plantations. How this attraction translates into dollars or pesos is, for now, anybody's guess.

Although CONAF recognizes the economic value of protected areas to tourism, broader discussions of forestry and forest resources often omit any reference to tourism or recreation dollars that these same resources provide to the national economy. The publication *Recursos Forestales de Chile* (CONAF, 1991) contains a useful overview of Chilean forests, briefly describes the major forest types and touts their increasing economic value, but only in terms of commodity production. Visitor expenditures and jobs generated by forest-related tourism and recreation are not mentioned. The appeal to international travelers of the giant alerce, the distinctive araucaria, the scarce hardwoods of the Bío-Bío region or the enchanted rainforests of the southern coast range are not addressed. Only in passing does the overview acknowledge that in national parks, flora, fauna and geological formations are of "educational, scientific or recreational interest."

The reader would presume that the economic benefits of keeping forests intact for tourism are either insignificant or of little interest to the public.

Chileans contacted in the course of this project, including some in the tourism industry, were unaware of any efforts on the part of government to correlate forests and tourism from an economic standpoint. It is entirely unclear how forest preservation and tourism might compete economically with resource exploitation, or what benefits might accrue in local communities if more forests were protected for tourists. Nevertheless, a few reasonable assumptions can be made. For instance, on any given plot of undeveloped native forest land, intensive timber harvest operations undoubtedly produce a high level of income per hectare compared to tourism, but only during the period in which the trees are cut. Adverse effects of intensive logging on water quality, fish and wildlife habitat, soils and other resources are often long-term problems that can be costly to adjacent landowners and the public at large. Traditionally, these costs have been ignored or underrated, and local economies as well as the natural heritage of the country suffer as a result.

A principal consideration is that environmentally and culturally responsible tourism can bring social, economic and environmental benefits to the same plot of land year after year, whereas lands that are heavily exploited are essentially removed from the tourism land base for decades, if not forever. Future economic studies and cost-benefit analyses need to reflect these factors.

Other developing countries have already substantiated the notion that preservation pays. The millions of hectares of protected rainforests in Costa Rica and Belize, set aside for all forest inhabitants, tourists included, are famous examples.[127] The International Union for the Conservation of Nature (IUCN) recently estimated that a lion in Kenya is worth $27,000 in tourist dollars each year.[128] An elephant herd is worth $610,000. If these species and their habitats are not protected, the costs to national economies would be tremendous. No comparable figures for Chilean species or habitats are known to exist although some striking figures could probably be developed. Adventure travel and research expeditions can pour thousands of dollars into cash-poor local economies each summer, money that would most likely be spent in another forest region in another country if Chile's temperate rainforests were not as intact as they are now.

While economic arguments are attractive to business people and bureaucrats, there are also terrific social and environmental rewards to be realized from ecotourism. Wild forests have strong potential to attract visitors, especially where properly designed facilities are available to access and appreciate them. When

Sustaining Communities & the Environment
(or Sustaining Investors?)

In the Alacalufes National Reserve near the southern tip of Chile, tourism and preservation may soon take a back seat to heavy industrial development. A giant aluminum plant and hydro-power dam proposed near the Strait of Magellan could destroy up to 7,000 hectares of productive forest and grazing lands important to local communities. Despite the promise of new jobs, residents are worried that the project will be severely damaging to tourism, forestry, the environment, and endangered species.[129]

To date, the Chilean government has supported nearly every multi-million or multi-billion-dollar multinational investment scheme to come along, regardless of the long-term social and environmental costs involved—and despite the fact that nature-oriented tourism has been increasing by leaps and bounds since the end of military rule in 1990. Throughout Chile, foreign investors continue to generate new proposals, consistently large-scale, damaging, disruptive, and of record-breaking proportions.

Yet many Chileans view the nation's southern reach as perhaps one of the best regions on Earth to establish a true model for sustainable living. The emergence of resource-consumptive mega-developments in the wildest regions of the globe is quite discouraging.

Above the siempreverde forest in the southern Andes.
❀ Ken Wilcox

people are able to experience wildness, they tend to value it more, and may be more inclined to help with preservation efforts. Native cultures who sometimes occupy these regions can be an excellent source of knowledge and insight on ecosystems and the potential for symbiosis between people and the forest environment. Although this presents a rare learning opportunity for travelers, respect for native cultures precludes unnecessary intrusions by casual tourists.

At the same time, some environmentalists insist that pristine areas will only be degraded where public access is improved. To be sure, large areas need to be preserved in a purely unaltered condition so that ecosystem integrity is not compromised. But if degradation from resource exploitation or development is a high risk in a given area—the Valdivian Rainforest, for example— ecotourism offers a very promising alternative for sustainable, non-destructive use of forest resources.

Finally, "ecotourism" is a frequently abused term that is often confused with "adventure travel." Some of the activities may be similar but the concepts are not the same. Simply lugging a daypack through a beautiful forest and saying we care is not enough. Real energy and personal commitment on the part of the travel industry and travelers alike are necessary to carry out truly environmentally responsible tourism.

With world-class tourism just beginning to develop in Chile, ecotourism could assume a powerful role in the protection of native forests. Much work needs to be done now to ensure long-term cultural and environmental sustainability in the link between forests and tourism. With over US$4 billion in foreign investments expected in Chile's forestry sector between 1992 and 1998, there is no time to lose.

How to be a Conscientious Eco-Traveler in Chile

Several highly respected international environmental organizations, including the World Resources Institute, the World Wildlife Fund and Conservation International, have produced good reports on the problems and promise of ecotourism in the developing world.[130] The benefits of protecting ecosystems, landscapes and native cultures are fundamental to each.

However, for those of us who might not have the time or inclination to delve into the technical details, the case studies or the economic aspects of ecotourism, the National Audubon Society[131] has suggested a simple "code of conduct" that tourists and tourism promoters might embrace:

- Do not disturb biotas.
- Make tourism resource-sustainable.
- Respect other cultures.
- Do not pollute.
- Educate yourself.
- Support the cause.
- Do not buy products that come from deleterious exploitation.

One item we might add is to think about where the money we spend is actually going. Who really benefits from a traveler's willingness to spend? Local people? Or are foreign guides, promoters or investors siphoning off the profits (the technical term is "leakage")? The World Bank estimates that globally, 55 cents of every tourism dollar spent in developing countries quickly "leaks" back to the industrialized nations.[132]

Also important to consider is whether our travel money is helping to protect ecosystems or achieve other local conservation objectives. If not, we can and should consider doing our spending somewhere else.

For more information on eco-tourism development in Chile, contact the National Tourism Service: SERNATUR, at Providencia 1550, Santiago, Chile.

4.5 A Secret Language

A BOOK SUCH AS THIS HAS NO REAL CONCLUSION, no final thoughts or ruminations about the beauty, source, and sanctity of the Chilean forest. Words do not easily capture these things — neither the grandeur nor the predicament. Yet in lieu of a final sweeping statement, some kind of parting remarks are in order.

Two writers, one Chilean, one Mapuche, offer a few thoughts regarding our historical relationship — and ancient, aboriginal dialogue — with the forest. If we can carry the essence of their words within ourselves and to those around us, perhaps we can convince the world that Chile's shrinking forests are, indeed, something to be concerned about.

Below, Adriana Hoffmann, an eminent Chilean botanist and ecologist, recaps the history of forest exploitation in Chile, setting the stage for an indigenous view of what the destruction means for our future relationship with the forest. In his brief essay, Ziley Mora, a respected Mapuche anthropologist, warns that nature's secret language is at stake.

Adriana Hoffmann...

The forests of Chile are formed of species which lived in tropical Gondwanaland, the enormous ancestral continent that comprised what is now South America, Africa, Australia and Antarctica, in a time when there were dinosaurs in Central Chile and forests covering the present northern deserts. After Gondwanaland separated into the continents we know today, these forests became isolated by impenetrable geographic barriers: the Andes, the Pacific Ocean, and the Atacama Desert. During the last glaciation the forests were restricted to small coastal areas of favorable climate where today exists the greatest biodiversity in the temperate world.

Humans seem to have inhabited this forest for over ten thousand years, yet their impact was almost always minimal. Upon the arrival of the Spanish in the mid-1500s, the vast

"...if a man loses one-third of his skin he dies... if a tree loses one-third of its bark it dies... Would it not be reasonable to suggest that if the Earth loses more than a third of its green mantle and tree cover, it will assuredly die?"

—Richard St. Barbe Baker
MY LIFE MY TREES [1970]

majority of central-southern Chile was covered with a dense and ancient cover of trees. The forest and the beings living there were respected by the Mapuche and other indigenous groups. Araucaria, canelo, and alerce trees were considered sacred.

Spanish and other Eurpoean colonists began to utilize and destroy the forest. They cut large trees for ships and building construction. Intentional fire opened up the land for agriculture. Until 1850 this impact was limited to central Chile. Immediately to the south, the Mapuche Nation kept these invaders out during the longest war in human history—over three hundred years. Ultimately, they were overcome and European colonization of the south began. Much of the coast range was burned and converted to wheat, later to be abandoned.

The forestry technique often applied was high-grading which, through removal of the best trees, continues to have a severe effect on the genetic health of native forests. Around 1940 large plantations of exotic pine and eucalyptus began appearing, planted in soils already degraded. Since the 1950s native forest destruction has continued unabated. In the far south millions of hectares of lenga forest were burned for cattle grazing. High rainfall, steep slopes, and poor management led to desertification of some areas following severe erosion.

Since 1988 the uncontrolled development of the wood chipping industry has left the Chilean people in confusion and bitter debate between those who think that maximum exploitation is sacrosanct, and those who promote conservation of natural resources and who know deforestation and consequent extinction of species to be an irreparable loss for the world.

Ziley Mora...

> The books of the old ones were the trees. From them they learned to read what would come to pass. Those above would use the trees as a pathway to bring down word of what was not seen. Before, there were special people who knew these secrets; that is why we, the few Mapuche who remain from the old days, do not need books nor writing. All the words from the beginning of the world have already been written.

These words, an indigenous manifesto for the preservation of forest, were transcribed from an ancient Mapuche, Abel Kuriwingka, in 1990 at 90 years of age. He died soon thereafter, having left his message as an emblem to embrace the cause of the great trees. His words contain the secret kept by the southernmost forest on Earth.

Today the notion of the immense, millennial, ancestral tree-as-oracle is all but lost to Western culture. The precolumbian view of the Mapuche regarding ancient trees as registers of energy circulating between Heaven and Earth is aligned with the Nordic tradition. "Book" and "tree" are one word in this early language.

The Mapuche conserve the truly Old World notion of the wisdom of the trees, far removed from Cartesian philosophy, even though the Spanish for tree, "arbol," comes from the Latin "arbor," which means "realm of the High Ones."

The disappearance of native forest, therefore, means the end of Nature's secret language—the absence of a code of wisdom that dignifies and enriches humankind.

A Conservation Legacy...

The destruction of native forests, *los arboles*, in Chile has, indeed, reached a crisis of national and even global importance. More than half the original forests are gone and half of what's left is seriously impaired or degraded—a legacy of greed and ignorance, perhaps a lack of vision. Thousands of hectares still vanish each day. But what remains (for the moment) includes some of the most unique, biologically diverse and majestic temperate forests on the planet. These forests, too, are a legacy.

Pablo Neruda's "fragrant, silent, tangled Chilean forest" survives today because there are people in Chile who care about nature and who believe healthy native forest ecosystems should not be sacrificed for the sake of maximizing short-term profits, nor lost to the "gigantic collective madness we are living," suggests Manfred Max Neef, Chilean environmentalist and Nobel Prize alternate.[133]

If we can learn to hear and understand the secret language of the forest—and the history of its decimation—there is, perhaps, a larger lesson for us all; a simple message that drifts like silence through an endless canopy of trees. In the words of Abel Kuriwingka:

All the Earth is One.
We are a part.
Our soul cannot die.
Change—it can!
But die—never!
One Soul are we.
Like one Earth.

CODEFF:
Comite Nacional pro-Defensa de la Fauna y Flora

The most prominent environmental organization in Chile is the National Committee for the Defense of Fauna and Flora, or CODEFF. It is the oldest environmental authority in the nation and the most successful in terms of lessening the impact of human society on the natural environment.

CODEFF has played a lead role in Chile on native forest issues, the conservation of biodiversity, air and water quality issues, marine mammal protection, hydropower development, indigenous peoples, the fate of Antarctica, and a host of other issues.

Staffed by competent researchers, scientists, political experts and volunteers, CODEFF has contributed immensely to the protection of alerce, araucaria and other forests, and has performed a number of studies concerning the impacts of people and plantations on native ecosystems.

The organization is known for its constructive and cooperative approach to problem-solving and has earned the respect of political leaders, agencies, institutions and the public at large, as well as the international environmental community.

CODEFF is nonprofit and based in Santiago with branch offices throughout the country. For more information (or to contribute to their efforts), write:

CODEFF
CASILLA 3675
SANTIAGO, CHILE

DEFENSORES DEL BOSQUE CHILENO
(Defendors of the Chilean Forest)

A rising star among Chilean environmental organizations, Defendors of the Chilean Forest is the only one solely dedicated to ecologically sustainable forestry and the preservation of native forests throughout Chile.

Under the leadership of renowned scientist-conservationist Adriana Hoffmann and a distinguished group of Chilean environmental leaders (Isabel Allende, Manfred Maxneef, Humberto Maturano, and others), *Defensores* has become a high-profile campaign with the goal of enlisting and activating one percent of the population on behalf of sound forest policy and practice.

The group is opposed to chipping native forests, or substituting them with plantations of exotic species. At the same time, *Defensores* supports the legal institutionalization of ecologically sustainable forestry, as well as incentives for protecting privately held ancient forest.

Defenders of the Chilean Forest is also nonprofit and based in Santiago with branch offices elsewhere in the country. For more information, write:

DEFENDERS OF THE CHILEAN FOREST
ANTONIA LÓPEZ DE BELLO 024
BELLAVISTA, SANTIAGO, CHILE

FUNDACIÓN LAHUEN
(Lahuen Foundation)

In response to the need for a nongovern-mental organization to oversee specific forest preservation projects in Chile, the Lahuen Foundation was formally established in Santiago in 1991. While environmental education and sustainable forestry alternatives are major objectives today, the foundation was originally set up to acquire, conserve and manage private lands deserving of protection, not unlike the Nature Conservancy.

Lahuen immediately began work on two unique projects: the Cañi, an araucaria preserve and environmental education center near Pucón, and Magdalena Island, a superb rainforest island ecosystem in the fiords of northern Patagonia. On Magdalena, a transfer of 35,000 hectares from CONAF to Lahuen was negotiated in support of research and conservation objectives.

The foundation is directed by a seven-member board comprised of leading representives from the scientific, business and environmental communities in Chile.

The Lahuen Foundation is also active in promoting sound national environmental and native forest policy and has lobbied effectively for change. In a time of massive foreign investment in Chilean resources, rapid growth in the forest industry, and a continuing expansion of exotic species plantations, the Lahuen Foundation has become a key organization for native forest awareness.

The name Lahuen comes from the Mapuche term for plants with healing qualities. For more information, write:

LAHUEN FOUNDATION
ORREGO LUCO 054
PROVIDENCIA, SANTIAGO, CHILE

BOSQUE ANTIGUO - CHILE
(Ancient Forest - Chile)

A nonprofit native forest research and education organization, Bosque Antiguo was established in 1991. It began in concert with several research expeditions into the Valdivian Rainforest organized with CODEFF and Ancient Forest International. The group was formed by university educators from various disciplines but with an emphasis on the social sciences.

Bosque Antiguo's goals are to investigate through credible research and expeditions the social and economic aspects of forestry and forest preservation, and to develop an ecological history of Chile's primary forests.

Like the others, the group is concerned with chipping and the conversion of native forests to non-native plantations, and supports the development of ecologically sustainable use of forests in Chile, including ecotourism.

Bosque Antiguo is also based in Santiago. For more information, write:

BOSQUE ANTIGUO - CHILE
CASSILLA 124, CORREO 58
ÑUÑOA, SANTIAGO, CHILE

FOUNDATION FOR EDUCATION, SCIENCE & ECOLOGY
(EDUCEC)

The Foundation for Education, Science and Ecology, directed by seven highly respected Chileans in the fields of conservation, science and law, was established to receive title to the 270,000 hectare fiordal sanctuary known as "Parque Pumalin," hailed as one of the most ambitious privately funded wilderness preservation efforts ever. The Foundation and the park were created by San Francisco businessman, Doug Tompkins, founder of Esprit and North Face, as well as the Foundation for Deep Ecology.

This pioneering conservation effort came about after several international expeditions into the northern fiords of Chilean Patagonia, organized by CODEFF, Bosque Antiguo and AFI. Tompkins was already impressed with the diversity and biomass of Chilean rainforests and has traveled through the country extensively both before and since the acquisition of Parque Pumalin.

In addition to land acquisition, the Foundation advocates for wildland preservation to ensure the long-term viability of all native forest ecosystems, and promotes ecotourism development as an alternative to conventional forest exploitation.

For more information, write:

FOUNDATION FOR EDUCATION,
SCIENCE & ECOLOGY
PROVIDENCIA, SANTIAGO, CHILE

ANCIENT FOREST INTERNATIONAL
(AFI)

AFI was established in 1989 as the only international environmental organization dedicated soley to the preservation of the world's temperate forest ecosystems, particularly temperate rainforests. Since embarking on several research expeditions into Chile's spectacular Valdivian Rainforest, the native forests of this unique southern nation have become a major focus for the group. Its efforts (one of which is this publication) have been highly effective in alerting the world to the problems of deforestation, opportunities for wildland preservation, as well as sustainable alternatives to conventional industrial forestry.

AFI has a strong working relationship with Chilean NGOs such as CODEFF, Defenders of the Chilean Forest, Lahuen Foundation, and others, while helping to secure lands in the Cañi, at Parque Pumalin, and elsewhere.

AFI's home is in the redwoods of northern California. For more information, write:

ANCIENT FOREST INTERNATIONAL
P. O. BOX 1850
REDWAY, CA 95560

CHILE INFORMATION PROJECT
(CHIP)

CHIP, an English language news service out of Santiago, was established in the 1980s by Steve Anderson to help disseminate news and dialogue from Chile to the rest of the world. To learn more about this excellent news source, contact Steve by e-mail at <anderson@chip.mic.cl>, or write to P. O. Box 53331, Correo Central, Santiago, Chile.

Notes & References

Part 1: Native Forests of Chile

1. Claudio Donoso, "Modificaciones del Paisaje Chileno a lo largo de la Historia," from the proceedings of a symposium: *Desarrollo y perspectivas de las Disciplinas forestales en la Universidad Austral de Chile.* University Austral, Valdivia, 1983. Large areas of sclerophyllous and roble-lingue-laurel forest in central Chile were also destroyed in the 19th century, due to an expanding population, concomitant land development and fuelwood collection, and even more importantly, the widespread clearing of lands for cultivating wheat. The damage can be correlated to extensive colonization by Europeans after 1855.

2. Brian Loveman, *Chile: The Legacy of Hispanic Capitalism.* Oxford University Press, Oxford, 1988. Also Dr. Cecil Corbett, Kurt Russo, Ed., "Revisiting Columbus" from *Our People... Our Land, Reflections on Common Ground: 500 Years.* Florence R. Kluckhohn Center & Lummi Indian Treaty Protection Task Force, Seattle, 1992. Similar figures are widely quoted in other publications.

3. Instituto Forestal (INFOR), *Estadísticas Forestales 1990.* INFOR, Santiago, 1991.

4. Conflicting figures appear in articles and other references used in this work. Standing forests are often estimated at 11 to 15 million hectares. The nation's nearly 14 million hectares of protected wildlands, which consist of vastly *non-forested* land (e.g. deserts, alpine areas, ice fields, etc.) administered by CONAF, are often confused with the amount of native forest present in Chile today. With the introduction of a new forest law in the Chilean Congress in 1992, CONAF estimated native forests at 14.6 million hectares (as reported in *El Mercurio* and other periodicals, April-July, 1992). This figure is consistent with estimates provided by Pablo Donoso (CODEFF, Valdivia) in 1991. Nevertheless, revised estimates can be expected as new forest surveys are conducted over the next several years.

5. Since AFI began its international campaign for forest conservation and wildland preservation in Chile, the issue has appeared on the agenda of a number of political, environmental, academic and industry organizations; in the U. S., news stories and essays have appeared in *National Geographic, Sierra,* The *New York Times,* the *San Francisco Chronicle,* and others; Chilean forests have also been the subject of scientific conferences within Chile and elsewhere, and articles have appeared in several technical journals. Sources used are noted later in this section. In an article entitled "Scientific cooperation with Chile" printed in the journal, *BioScience* (Vol. 40 No. 8), S. T. A. Pickett and J. J. Armesto write: "The importance and diversity of temperate ecosystems in South America have been scarcely recognized. Yet knowledge of South American temperate forests and freshwaters is important both ecologically and for understanding the impact of global environmental change."

6. César S. Ormazábal, "Threatened Plant Sites and Vegetation Types in Chile. A Proposal," from *Red List of Chilean Terrestrial Flora.* Iván L. Benoit, Ed., CONAF, Santiago, 1989. Ormazábal states: "The responsibility of Chile regarding protection of her flora heritage is immense. While the number of vascular plant species proper of this country amounts to 5,215 (including a small number of naturalized species)–grouped in 192 families and 1,032 genera (Marticorena & Quezada, 1985)–may seem small in comparison with the number of species in large-sized countries with tropical rainforests, the degree of endemism, i.e. plants occurring naturally only within the Chilean territory, is extremely high; according to Gajardo (1983) and IUCN (1986), it exceeds 50 percent."

7. Claudio Donoso, "Investigación y desarrollo forestal." CONAF, Santiago, 1981.

8. Rodolfo Gajardo, *Sistema Básico de Clasificación de la Vegetación Nativa Chilena.* University of Chile & CONAF, Santiago, 1983.

9. Claudio Donoso (1981), op. cit.

10. Carolina Zegers, Hernán Verscheure & Gabriel Sanhueza, *El Futuro del Bosque Nativo Chileno: Un Desafío de Hoy.* CODEFF, Santiago, October 1992.

11. Francisco Ulloa, "Alcances sobre la disponibilidad del bosque nativo comercial en Chile," *Actas XI Jornadas Forestales.* Colegio de Ingenieros Forestales, University of Chile, Santiago, 1984.

12. Iván Benoit, "Araucaria: Patrimonio en Peligro," *Biosfera Magazine.* Santiago, April 1992. The estimate of 50,000 hectares of pure araucaria stands that exist today is based on discussions with CODEFF representatives in Chile.

13. Spencer B. Beebe & Edward C. Wolf, "The Coastal Temperate Rainforest: An Ecosystem Management Perspective," *Coastal Watersheds: An Inventory of Watersheds in the Coastal Temperate Forests of British Columbia.* Earthlife Canada Foundation & Ecotrust/Conservation International, Vancouver, 1991. The authors point out: "On a global scale, coastal temperate rain forests are relatively rare. The temperate forest biome in general covers

some 1.3 billion hectares, or nine percent of the earth's land area. But only 31 million hectares of this is classifiable as coastal temperate rain forest, which amounts to 2.4 percent of the temperate forest, and 0.2 percent of the planet's land area. By comparison, tropical rain forests originally encompassed slightly more than two billion hectares, or 14 percent of the earth's land area — of which by most accounts one-half has been destroyed... What remains of unlogged, natural coastal temperate rain forests has yet to be calculated, but it is obviously diminished from its original range — probably by one-half as well."

14. Paul Alaback, "Comparative ecology of temperate rainforests of the Americas along analogous climatic gradients." USDA Forest Service, Juneau, 1990. Also Paul Alaback & James Weigand, "The Status of Temperate Rainforest in British Columbia." Conservation International & Earthlife Canada Foundation, Vancouver, December 1990. In the latter the authors write: "Because of the absence of fire and other frequent large-scale natural catastrophes, temperate rainforests are very old and the trees tend to be large... [They] usually accumulate and store more organic matter and wood volume than tropical rainforests. They can accumulate as much as 500-2,000 metric tons of organic matter per hectare. There are large amounts of organic debris and litterfall on the ground which accumulate and persist over centuries. Thick carpets of ferns and mosses often cloak the forest floor."

15. J. D. Ovington, Ed., *Ecosystems of the World, Vol. 10: Temperate Broad-Leaved Evergreen Forests.* Elsevier, New York, 1983.

16. Spencer B. Beebe, "Conservation in Temperate and Tropical Rain Forests: The Search for an Ecosystem Approach to Sustainability." Conservation International/Ecotrust, Portland, 1991. Estimates will likely be revised in the near future as native forest inventories underway in Chile (1994-97) begin to produce more reliable figures.

17. Calvin J. Heusser, "Vegetation and Climate of the Southern Chilean Lake District During and Since the Last Interglaciation," *Quaternary Research 4.* University of Washington, Seattle, 1974.

18. Paul Alaback (1990), op. cit.

19. Ibid.

20. Claudio Donoso (1981), op. cit.

21. Ibid. Also J. D. Ovington, op cit.

22. Claudio Donoso (1981), op. cit.

23. Antonio Lara & Ricardo Villalba, "A 3620-Year Temperature Record from *Fitzroya cupressoides* Tree Rings in Southern South America," *Science,* 21 May 1993. The authors explain: "Our 3622-year temperature reconstruction [from tree ring analysis] is currently the longest annually resolved climate reconstruction from tree rings. In addition, this study demonstrates that alerce may live over 3600 years, which makes it the second longest living tree after bristlecone pine (*Pinus longaeva*)."

24. CODEFF, "Information on the State of Conservation of the Species Alerce (*Fitzroya cupressoides*) in Chile, Supporting the Argentine Proposal Submitted to CITES 1987." This document offers a summary of the population and distribution of alerce in Chile and Argentina, and sums up legal protective measures that have been taken as follows: "Legal protection of the species is based mainly on the Supreme Decree 490 of 1st October, 1976, which accorded the alerce the status of Natural Monument, recognizing its value as a national heritage of scientific, historical and cultural importance. The Decree prohibits the cutting of live trees but permits the logging of dead specimens. This has been a loophole of serious consequences because it has caused the killing of alerce trees by intentionally set fires and different other methods, like cutting a ring in the bark, in order to log them "legally"... [The Decree was delayed] so that logging companies had ample time to cut all the trees they wanted before the prohibition came into force... In international commerce the species is mainly protected by CITES which was ratified by Chile in 1975. From the beginning both the Chilean and the Argentine alerce populations were included in Appendix I... The U. S. put the alerce in December 1979 on the list of the Endangered Species Act..."

25. Claudio Donoso (1983), op. cit.

26. *El Mercurio* (Santiago, September 5, 1994) reported the establishment of the world's largest privately financed forest and wildlife reserve in Palena Province southeast of Puerto Montt. The project, "Parque Pumalin," is sponsored by The Education, Science, and Ecology Foundation (EDUCEC) and includes 270,000 hectares of wildlands near the Comao Glacier. The acquisition was largely funded by environmental interests in the United States, including a $3 million donation from Doug Tompkins. Tompkins spokesperson, Daniel Gonzalez, expects the reserve to produce jobs in tourism and noted that the project is consistent with public policy that encourages private initiatives in the protection of natural areas. The land includes substantial areas of ancient siempreverde and alerce forest.

27. Iván Benoit, an endangered species expert with CONAF in Santiago, expressed the urgency of protecting all species in this globally unique environment (during a 1992 interview with the author).

28. Claudio Donoso, *Ecología Forestal: El Bosque y su Medio Ambiente.* Editorial Universitaria, Santiago, 1990.

29. Claudio Donoso (1990), op. cit.

30. Claudio Donoso (1990), op. cit. Donoso writes: "At the end of 1958 and the beginning of 1959 there were so many fires in southern Chile that visibility was reduced to one kilometer due to the smoke that rose to great altitudes in enormous columns, and covered the territory from mountain range to mountain range... Only a strong rain that fell in the beginning of February put an end to this veritable tragedy."

31. Juan Armesto, Santiago, shared this comment during a review of the manuscript for this book (March 1993).

32. Claudio Donoso (1990), op. cit.

33. Claudio Donoso (1990), op. cit.

34. Alfonso A. Glade, Ed., *Red List of Chilean Terrestrial Vertebrates*. CONAF, Santiago, 1988.

35. J. D. Ovington (1983), op. cit.

36. J. D. Ovington (1983), op. cit.

37. Alex Frid, "Magellanic Forests of Southernmost Chile: A Mythical Wilderness No More?" Undated manuscript (~1991-92).

38. Proposed aluminum smelters and hydroelectric power projects have been reported in several periodicals including *El Mercurio* (12 March 1991, 23 March 1992, 2 June 1992, and 23 October 1992, as reported by CHIP, the Chile Information Project). The "Alumysa" project, proposed by Noranda of Canada and Nissho of Japan, is a huge aluminum smelter and hydroelectric dam planned for the Cuervo River near Puerto Chacabuco. At $1.6 billion, it would be the largest private development in Chilean history. The project relies on alumina shipped from Australia where adverse economic impacts will hit the hardest. Cheap labor and energy (both of which generally ignore most long-term social and environmental costs) have investors excited over the prospect of substantial short-term profits. CODEFF is concerned with not only the massive alterations to the natural landscape this project promises, but the highly contaminant hydrocarbons that would be released to the air, and the discharge of liquid wastes containing heavy metals, sulphur and oil into adjacent waters, putting both marine and aquatic ecosystems as well as the net-pen salmon industry at risk. Two other large aluminum projects have also been announced, including another in the Aisén region, and a potential $2 billion facility near Punta Arenas in the far south. Endesa, Chile's quasi-public utility giant who is spearheading the development of six dams on the Bío-Bío River, has been negotiating for a piece of the action. Endesa also hopes to install two dams on another spectacular river, the Futaleufú, for even more power production.

39. Alex Frid (undated), op. cit.

Part 2: Forest Exploitation

40. Charles Darwin, *Voyage of the Beagle*. Bantam Books edition, New York, 1972.

41. Ibid.

42. An illustrious naturalist in his own regard, Alexander von Humboldt exerted a major influence on Darwin in the years prior to his round-the-world voyage on the H.M.S. Beagle. Humboldt traveled through South America from 1799 until 1804, later producing six volumes of work entitled *Personal Narrative: Travels to the Equinoctial Regions of the New Continent 1799-1804* (1819). Some years later, Darwin explained in his autobiography (1858) that Humboldt's narrative "stirred up in me a burning zeal to add even the most humble contribution to the noble structure of Natural Science. No one or a dozen other books influenced me nearly so much as these two," referring also to John Herschel's *Preliminary Discourse on the Study of Natural Philosophy* (1831). He was particularly excited by the notion of going to the Canary Islands to experience the fantastic and unfamiliar world of tropical vegetation. He writes: "...my enthusiasm is so great that I cannot hardly sit still on my chair." (Quoted in *Charles Darwin: A New Life*, by John Bowlby, W. W. Norton & Company, New York, 1990.)

43. Charles Darwin (1972), op. cit.

44. Pablo Donoso, *Diagnóstico de la situación actual del bosque nativo en Chile* (January 1991). Donoso presented this highly researched and enlightened report to the Environmental Commission of Congress' Chamber of Deputies for their consideration in deliberating a new forest law.

45. Claudio Donoso (1983), op. cit.

46. Claudio Donoso (1983), op. cit. See also Jose Bengoa, *Historia del Pueblo Mapuche*, Ediciones Sur/Colección Estudios Historicos, Santiago, 1987; Junius Bird, John Hyslop, ed.,*Travels and Archaeology in South Chile*, University of Iowa Press, Iowa City, 1988; John Cooper, *The Araucanians: Handbook of South American Indians, Vol. 2.*, Washington, 1946; Tom Dillahay, *Estudios Antropológicos Sobre Los Mapuches de Chile Sur-Central*, Universidad Catolica, Temuco, 1976; L. C. Faron, *The Mapuche Indians of Chile*, Holt, Rinehart and Winston, New York, 1968; Brian Loveman, *Chile: The Legacy of Hispanic Capitalism*, Oxford University Press, Oxford, 1988; Vicente Mariqueo, *The Mapuche Tragedy*, IWGIA, Copenhagen, 1979; H. R. S. Pocock, *The Conquest of Chile*, Stein and Day, New York, 1967; Osvaldo Silva, *Atlas Historia de Chile*, Editorial Universitaria, Santiago, 1983; Osvaldo Silva,

Culturas y Pueblos de Chile Prehispano, Editorial Salesiana, Santiago, 1990; Sergio Villalobos, et al, *Historia de Chile*, Editorial Universitaria, Santiago, 1990.

47. Instituto Forestal (INFOR), *Estadisticas Forestales 1993*. INFOR, Santiago, 1994.

48. See *Ambiente y Desarrollo*, "Aserraderos Copihue: protección de suelos, control de dunas y recuperación de flora y fauna, entre las prioridades ambientales," by Guillermo Güell (CIPMA, Santiago, August 1990); *Chile País Forestal*, "Aventuras y Desventuras del Bosque Chileno," Hernán Cortés, Editor (CORMA, Santiago, July 1991); and "Avances en suelos y nutrición forestales," by Juan E. Schlatter in the proceedings of the symposium: *Desarrollo y perspectivas de las Disciplinas forestales en la Universidad Austral de Chile* (University Austral, Valdivia, 1983).

49. Pablo Donoso (1991), op. cit.; also INFOR (1991-94), op. cit.

50. Pablo Donoso, "Definición de alternativas de manejo y conservación para el bosque nativo de Chile sur-central," CODEFF/World Wildlife Fund, Santiago, 1993.

51. *Chile Forestal*, CONAF, Santiago, 1990-91.

52. Brian Loveman (1988), op. cit.

53. Adriana Hoffmann, *Flora Silvestre de Chile: Zona Araucana, 2nd Edition*. Ediciones Fundación Claudio Gay, Santiago, 1991; Claudio Donoso (1990), op. cit.

54. INFOR (1991), op. cit.

55. INFOR (1991), op. cit.

56. Pablo Donoso (1991) op. cit.; Pablo Donoso, "El Consumo de Leña en Chile," CODEFF, Santiago, 1989.

57. Hernán Cortés, "Impacto de la producción en los bosques naturales," and Juan Franco, "El rol del Estado en el manejo del patrimonio forestal nativo," in *Ambiente y Desarrollo* (CIPMA, Santiago, August 1990). Franco notes that the production of wood fiber within degraded native forests could be increased dramatically, offering "enormous potential" if these areas were managed more thoughtfully.

58. INFOR (1995), op. cit.; CHIP.

59. The Chile Information Project (CHIP) reported Trillium's plans for Rio Condor in January 1994, and added "Trillium is giving the appearance of a sincere attempt at enlightened forestry." On April 20, 1994, *El Mercurio* reported that the President of the House Environmental and Natural Resources Committee in Chile's Congress was calling for a moratorium against cutting lenga forests in the far south. After visiting the area, the Deputy recommended a revocation of Trillium's management plan and suggested a regional plebiscite to gauge citizen support for large-scale cutting of lenga forests. CHIP also reported a story in *El Mercurio* on October 31, 1995, in which Claudio Donoso, a widely respected forest ecologist and member of the Rio Condor Scientific Commission, states: "If Trillium should deceive us, something I doubt very much since we have been working with them for two years, we at the [Commission] would be the first to denounce them." The author's lingering skepticism concerning the company's plans for Rio Condor is based on several factors, including the large-scale nature of the development (a small city, shipping port and power generation facilities will be constructed in a remote location to accommodate a project which appears to be getting bigger over time — Trillium investors apparently doubled their holdings in Tierra del Fuego in late 1994 by acquiring a large area of forest on the Argentine side of the border). Trillium has also resisted implementing its own *Stewardship Principles* (developed for Rio Condor) in managing the company's considerable holdings in its home territory in northwest Washington State. Instead, the company argues that clearcut logging methods are the best choice, and necessary to correct poor forestry practices in the past. In a full-page ad placed in a local conservative newspaper, Trillium states: "We have been encouraged by the support our plans have received from the Chilean government and from the people in the region. The key to their support is our commitment to sustainability — sustainability in the broadest definition of the word: sustainability of the resource, the economic benefit to Chileans, and the ecosystem" (*Bellingham Herald*, December 1, 1994). However, the Stewardship Principles (included in the ad) state something a little different: "The Project's forests will be responsibly managed for indefinitely sustainable hardwood production, using the best available scientific knowledge to assure the protection of both the ecosystem and the well being of those associated with the project. To this end, the average annual rate of harvest during any ten year period will not exceed levels that support an indefinitely sustainable harvest." The notion of sustainability of the forest ecosystem, one of the greatest concerns of the environmental community in both Chile and the Pacific Northwest, is qualified by the statement "Short term compromises may be required in economic productivity, environmental protection or social welfare, but these compromises will be made only in the context of a realistic plan for the long term balance of all of these values." No one can predict how Trillium will put its words into action, or whether the rustlings at Rio Condor are a sincere prelude to "enlightened forestry," or just another scheme to convert magnificent wildlands into short term corporate profits. Ultimately, the project may be less damaging to some elements of the environment than the more conventional approach to industrial forestry, and that aspect should certainly be encouraged. Trillium's (and CEO David Syre's) willingness to work closely with

Chilean ecologists, incorporate their recommendations, and establish protected reserves in key areas (thanks in part to the constructive prodding of Bellingham environmental attorney, Rand Jack), is commendable and makes Rio Condor a hopeful precedent for a more thoughtful approach to forestry in Chile. It may not, however, be a perfect model for *ecologically sustainable forestry*, a key concern that should not be confused in the discussion of sustainable *harvests*. To explore this issue further, consult: "What Should Forests Sustain? Eight answers" by Richard P. Gale and Sheila M. Corday (*Journal of Forestry*, May 1991); "Rol de la Ciencia y la Tecnología en el Desarrollo Sustenable del Sector Forestal: Una visión desde los organismos no gubernamentales," by Aarón Caveres (CODEFF, Santiago, undated report); "Integrating Biological Diversity and Resource Management," by John R. Probst and Thomas R. Crow (*Journal of Forestry*, February 1991); and "Conservation in Temperate and Tropical Rain Forests: The Search for an Ecosystem Approach to Sustainability," by Spencer B. Beebe (Conservation International/Ecotrust, Portland, 1991).

60. *Chile Forestal*, CONAF, Santiago, 1991.

61. CODEFF, "Posición de CODEFF sobre el proyecto forestal Corral de la empresa Terranova (CAP/Marubeni), position paper, Santiago, 1990; Veronica Rodriguez, "Maximiliano Cox: 'Terranova sentara un precedente... sera la fijación de una politica'," *Chile Forestal*, CONAF, Santiago, September 1990.

62. Iván Benoit (1989), op. cit.

63. Ibid. See also A. Cabeza, "Aspectos históricos de la legislación vinculada la conservación, la evolución de las áreas silvestres de la zona de Villarica y la creación del primer parque nacional de Chile," CONAF, Santiago, 1988.

64. Iván Benoit (1989), op. cit.

65. Eladio Susaeta and Susana Benedetti, "El sector forestal y la conservación ambiental," *Ambiente y Desarrollo* (CIPMA, Santiago, August 1990); George B. Harpole, "Forest Resources," in *Forest Products from Latin America* (USDA Forest Service, Madison, March 1991). The latter notes that throughout Latin America "plantation harvest is expected to increase almost tenfold by the year 2030" to 342 million cubic meters, up from 36 million in 1985. Wood production from radiata pine in Chile was projected to increase fivefold in 15 years (1985 to 2000).

66. *El Mercurio*, Santiago, January 22, 1993 (from CHIP news service).

67. F. Hartwig, "Visión del desarrollo forestal de Chile," Santiago, 1989 (cited by César S. Ormazábal in "The Conservation of Biological Diversity in Chile," unpublished, Yale University, December 1990).

68. *El Mercurio*, Santiago, December 14, 1991 (from CHIP news service). The comment is attributed to Efrain Antriao who also expressed concern with indiscriminate logging in the region.

69. *El Mercurio*, Santiago, January 23, 1993 (from CHIP news service). The report states "Indigenous leader Jose Santos Millao announced that he will call for a national plebiscite if indigenous groups in Chile are not recognized by the Constitution as a separate 'people'. Santos Millao declared that all the help offered by the Government amounts to little, when compared with the enormous historical debt which Chile owes the indigenous population. However, he admitted that the new law is an important step forward..."

Part 3: Forest Conservation

70. Carlos A. Weber, "Chile," in the *International Handbook of National Parks and Nature Reserves*, Greenwood Press, New York, 1990. Albert, according to Weber, "waged an unceasing campaign aimed at the conservation of renewable resources, a campaign that resulted in establishment of the first fish-farming operations, stabilization of shifting sand dunes, planting of forests, and the creation of national parks and forest reserves," despite the fact that "environmental awareness in Chile was very low at the turn of the century."

71. César S. Ormazábal (1990), op. cit.

72. World Resources Institute, *World Resources 1990-91*, Oxford University Press, New York, 1990.

73. Pablo Donoso (1991), op. cit.

74. Carlos Weber, in an interview with the author, 1992.

75. César S. Ormazábal (1990), op. cit. Similar data for invertebrates and inferior plants is generally lacking.

76. Rick Klein, AFI, 1992.

77. *El Mercurio*, Santiago, June 11, 1993 (from CHIP news service). The report notes: "Although its original habitat extended from Valparaíso to Chiloé, [the copihue] has become increasingly scarce due to soil erosion, the change in climate, and the substitution of native forests."

78. Sandra Postel and Lori Heise, "Reforesting the Earth," *Worldwatch Paper 83*, Worldwatch Institute, April 1988.

79. World Resources Institute, *World Resources 1988-89*, Oxford University Press, New York, 1988.

80. M. D. F. Uvardy, "A biogeographical classification system for terrestrial environments," proceedings of the 1982 World Congress on National Parks, Smithsonian Institution Press, Washington D. C., 1984.

81. Uvardy (1984) op. cit., cited in Ormazábal (1990), op. cit.

82. IGM, *Atlas geográfico de Chile para la educación*, Instituto Geográfico Militar, Santiago, 1988, cited in Ormazábal (1990), op. cit.

83. E. O. Wilson, "The current state of biological diversity," National Academy Press, Washington D. C., 1988, and T. L. Erwin, "Tropical Forest: Their richness in coleoptera and other arthropod species" in *Coleoptera Bulletin*, V. 36 No. 1, 1982 (both cited in Ormazábal (1990), op. cit.).

84. César S. Ormazábal (1990), op. cit.

85. Rodolfo Gajardo (1983), op. cit. (cited in Ormazábal (1990), op. cit.).

86. R. Rodríguez, O. Matthei, and M. Quezada, "Flora arbórea de Chile," Editorial Universidad de Concepción, Concepción, 1983 (cited in Ormazábal (1990), op. cit.).

87. C. Marticorena and M. Quezada, "Catálogo de la flora vascular de Chile," Universidad de Concepción, Concepción, 1985 (cited in Ormazábal (1990), op. cit.).

88. Iván Benoit (1989), op. cit.

89. M. Tamayo, H. Nuñez and Yáñez, "Lista sistemática actualizada de los mamíferos vivientes en Chile y sus nombres comunes," National Museum of Natural History, Santiago, 1987 (cited in Ormazábal (1990), op. cit.).

90. Alfonso A. Glade (1988), op. cit.

91. V. Bullen, WWF-USA Southern Cone Program: Draft Country Plan: Chile, World Wildlife Fund (US), Washington, D. C., 1990 (cited in Ormazábal (1990), op. cit.).

92. David Herbst, in a letter to AFI following the 1991 expedition.

93. Alfonso Glade, *La Protección del Patrimonio Ecológico*, CONAF, Santiago, 1989. Efforts to enhance populations of black-necked swans, a vulnerable species, at Laguna Torca National Reserve on the coast of Region VII have also been successful. Only 296 swans were counted in 1979. Their numbers had grown to 717 by 1988 and they were beginning to occupy new areas in the reserve. Similar programs aimed at increasing scant populations of huemul, chinchilla and loro tricahue have not been so successful.

94. César S. Ormazábal (1990), op. cit.

95. *Chilean Forestry News*, "First seed orchard for native species," CONAF, Santiago, April 1990 (cited in César S. Ormazábal (1990), op. cit.).

96. César S. Ormazábal (1990), op. cit.; Iván Benoit (1989), op. cit. All three species are endemic to Regions VII and/or VIII where both the spread of pine plantations and the destruction of native forests have been most dramatic.

97. Antonio Lara & Ricardo Villalba (1993), op. cit.

98. John Krebs, "Monterey Pine: An Introduced Species in Chile," Publications in Climatology, Elmer, 1976. It is remarkable that Krebs' comment appears only two years after Decree Law 701 was enacted, creating an incentives program that led to the rapid development of plantations across central Chile. Since 1976 the total area of plantations has increased more than 1,000 percent (tenfold).

99. CORMA, "Inserción de Latinoamérica en el Comercio Mundial de Pulpa y Papel," *CORMA*, (No. 224), Santiago, January/February 1992.

100. César S. Ormazábal (1990), op. cit.; Iván Benoit (1989), op. cit.

101. Antonio Lara & Ricardo Villalba (1993), op. cit.; CODEFF (1987), op. cit.

Part 4: Future Forests

102. The list of sites was provided to the author by Adriana Hoffmann and reflects the priorities of many Chilean experts in biodiversity conservation.

103. *La Epoca*, June 2, 1992 (reported by CHIP). One thousand people around the country were questioned (40% in the Santiago metropolitan area). The poll was coordinated with similar polls in other countries which were carried out in conjunction with the 1992 Earth Summit in Rio de Janeiro.

104. *El Mercurio*, June 25, 1992 (reported by CHIP). Eleven hundred people in Santiago, Concepción and Valdivia were interviewed in the poll sponsored by CORMA (Chilean Wood Corporation).

105. *El Mercurio*, April 18, 1993 (reported by CHIP). According to the report, CODEFF's work "produced evidence of severe damage to native forests, either due to complete deforestation or to the selected cutting of highest quality trees, leaving insufficient numbers for the forest to recover." CODEFF also spoke to "the inefficiency of the courts of justice, who minimize the accusations made by [CONAF], thus permitting forestry companies to continue the devastation without being fined for the ecological damage they cause."

106. Presently, the term "sustainability" is being construed in as many ways as there are people using it to make a point. In *The War Against the Greens* (Sierra Club Books, San Francisco, 1994), writer David Helvarg observes: "The Washington buzzword of the moment, a free-trade import from the Rio Earth Summit, is

sustainable development, the idea that we can meet our economic needs today without compromising the quality of life for future generations. I hear it used repeatedly by administration officials, environmentalists, trade union leaders, corporate executives, and anti-enviro activists who see it as yet another preservationist plot to undermine the free-enterprise system... Sustainable development, like sustainable growth, may be something of an oxymoron, a consensus-building term that everyone can agree on as long as its implementing language remains largely undefined."

107. Ryan continues: "No single set of policy prescriptions will work to reconcile diverse societies and varied ecosystems to each other. No monolithic biodiversity commission can be charged with caretaking life for the world. The key will be an array of local approaches, informed by experiences in other places and supported by policies at higher levels... To intelligently limit the amount of the planet we dominate, and to tolerate diversity more in the places we do dominate, will entail tackling two of the most intractable and fundamental forces in the modern world: galloping per-capita consumption and rapid population growth. No conservation strategy, however ingenious, can get around the fact that the more resources one species consumes, the fewer are available for all the rest... much of the devastation of Southern economies and ecosystems is driven by Northern consumption of their resources, inequities of trade, debt and perhaps most important of all, overconsumption by wealthy nations and individuals... life on Earth transcends economics, even though economic insights can help choose effective means of halting biological losses. No price can be assigned to the ability of the atmosphere, forests, and oceans together to maintain a life-giving climate; no value can be assigned to a species that has endured for millions of years. Moreover, a viable relationship with the myriad parts and processes of the biosphere lies not so much in any economic sacrifice *for* them as in a recognition of our dependence *on* them, and a willingness to let this insight guide all our activities. Making the conservation of diversity a goal in everything we do would indeed be a fundamental shift. But anything less would be an abdication of our obligation to pass on to future generations a world of undiminished options, and of our moral responsibility as travelers on the only planet known to support life."

108. *El Mercurio*, June 14, 1992 (reported by CHIP).

109. World Resources Institute (1990), op. cit.; also Fernando Bascur, "Plan de Acción Forestal para América Latina y el Caribe," *Chile Forestal, Technical Document #47*, CONAF, Santiago, August 1990.

110. *El Mercurio*, February 1992 (reported by CHIP).

111. *El Mercurio*, July 5, 1992 (reported by CHIP).

112. *El Mercurio*, July 17, 1992 (reported by CHIP).

113. *El Mercurio*, July 15, 1993 (reported by CHIP).

114. *La Epoca*, February 28 , 1992 (reported by CHIP). President Aylwin's Finance Minister, Alexandro Foxley, explained that the Initiative program was open to creative and innovative ideas from non-governmental organizations.

115. El Mercurio, May 8, 1992 (reported by CHIP).

116. Pablo Donoso (1991), op. cit.

117. Ibid.

118. Pablo Donoso, in a 1992 interview with the author.

119. *La Epoca* (1992), op. cit.

120. *Euromonitor*, "World Market for Travel and Tourism," 1992 (cited in El Mercurio, June 13, 1992 and reported by CHIP).

121. For more detailed information concerning trends in ecotourism in Chile, contact SERNATUR, the National Tourism Service, in Santiago.

122. Carlos Weber (1990), op. cit.

123. Reported in *El Mercurio*, June 16, 1991. Tourism worldwide represented more than five percent of all salaries and generated about $2.5 billion a year. No information was available concerning the number of people employed specifically in ecotourism or adventure travel as a proportion of the overall industry.

124. *El Mercurio*, August 15, 1994 (reported by CHIP).

125. Carlos Weber (1990), op. cit.

126. *El Mercurio*, June 16, 1991.

127. David Quammen, "The Economy of Nature," *Outside*, February 1992.

128. *Audubon*, "Two Faces of Eco-Tourism," March 1990, National Audubon Society, New York. See also *earthTrips: a guide to nature travel on a fragile planet*, (Dwight Holing/Conservation International, Living Planet Press, Venice CA, 1991).

129. *El Mercurio*, August 3, 1992 (reported by CHIP).

130. See Kreg Lindberg, "Policies for Maximizing Nature Tourism's Ecological and Economic Benefits," World Resources Institute; Karen Ziffer, "Ecotourism: The Uneasy Alliance," Conservation International; Elizabeth Boo,

"Ecotourism: The Potentials and Pitfalls," World Wildlife Fund; "Tourism and Ecology: The Impact of Travel on a Fragile Earth," Center for Responsible Tourism.

131. *Audubon* (March 1990), op. cit.

132. David Quammen (1992), op. cit.

133. *El Mercurio*, August 24, 1995 (reported by CHIP). As an independent, Max Neef made a run for the Presidency of Chile in 1994 and came in an impressive third with about five percent of the vote. In a March 16, 1993 interview with *El Diario*, Max Neef commented: "We are following a seductive economic model that is unsustainable in the long-run. The model is unsustainable for biological, ecological, and thermodynamic reasons. The economy is a sub-system of a larger system that imposes contradictory restrictions... [To] become global in scope does not mean to sell to the whole world... We are becoming increasingly dependent upon an international market on which we have no influence whatsoever... we are becoming more impoverished. The GNP is calculated with a primitive methodology that adds up everything. It's as if you considered part of your steady income the money you receive for selling all your furniture. The nation has grown on a foundation of depredation. If you were to fly over our forests, you would be shocked at the degree and speed of the destruction. Eight years more along the same course will find the country totally devastated. I have the impression that officials are aware of the problem but don't know what to do about it. They lack even the willingness to reconsider their economic theory, based on doctrines disinterred from the neo-classic graveyard. While people of the industrialized world gradually come around, taking a despairing look at the world we have built and begin to ask how to get out of this mess, we throw ourselves head first into it, living the illusion of the GNP figures... Chile has the capability, if it wishes to use it, to begin drafting the design for a new economy. We could be like the Scandinavian countries which were the poorest of Europe eighty years ago. They felt compelled to create their own model and now they are the only nations where poverty has been banished. Chile could make a contribution of universal value. It would be an adventure worth taking."

About the author...

Ken Wilcox is an environmental writer and consultant who makes his home in Bellingham, Washington, on the edge of the North Cascades temperate rainforest. As a traveler to most of the forest regions described in this book, he has had the good fortune of meeting many of the people whose work and concern for Chile's forests are making a huge difference (and without whom this work would not have been possible).

In 1990-91 Ken participated with AFI on two research expeditions to Chile's Valdivian Rainforest; thoroughly enamored with the place, he vows to return as an avid ecotourist, if not life-long student of the Chilean forest.

In addition to this work and a local guidebook to recreation, Ken has a background in environmental policy, coastal management and wildland recreation. He has written articles on temperate rainforests and international environmental issues for several publications.

Index

Cape Horn 111
Caramávida 110
carpintero negro 104
Carretera Austral 123
Cauquenes 110
cellulose 55, 56
Central Bank (of Chile) 46
Central Chile xii (*map*), 10 (*map*), 11-18, 77, 84, 87, 109
Cerro Santa Lucia 67
Cerro Camaraca 112
Cerro Cayumanqui 110
Cerro Nombre 111
Cerros Los Molles 111
Chacabuco River Valley 111
Charles Darwin 43
Chilauna 111
Chile Information Project (CHIP) vii, 134
Chile's national flower 84
Chilean burrowing parrot 95
Chilean Congress 49, 70
Chilean independence 2
Chilean palm 1, 13, 61, 67, 77, 81, 84, 90
Chilean Patagonia 37, 71, 75, 83, 87
Chilean pigeon 95
Chilean woodstar 95
Chiloé 24, 26, 45, 46, 111, 117
Chiloé coihue 26, 41, 61
Chiloé colocolo opossum 93
Chiloé fox 93
Chiloé National Park 28, 91
chinchilla 93
Chinchilla laniger 93
CHIP (Chile Information Project) vii, 134
chipping industry 52, 55, 58, 117, 119
Cholchol River 111
Chonos Archipelago 24, 40, 41
Chonos people iii, 39, 45
choroy parrot 35
Choshuenco 110
chucao 35
chupalla 34
Chusquea quila 16
ciprés de la cordillera 14
ciprés de la cordillera forest 8, 10 (*map*), 14
ciprés de las Guaitecas forest 8, 36 (*map*), 41
Clarillo River 112
Claro River 110
climate 4, 12, 14, 16, 22, 33, 75, 84-88, 103, 113
Clinton/Gore administration 117
cloudforests 85
coast redwood 27, 30, 31
coastal mountains 11, 12, 14, 16, 22, 24, 26, 37, 101, 109
coastal degu 93
CODEFF (Comite Nacional pro Defensa de la Fauna y Flora) vii, x, 27, 28, 47, 48, 56, 68, 69, 89, 100, 114, 119, 132
coihue 13, 21, 22, 24-28, 30, 33, 34, 37, 39, 40, 42, 46, 61, 103, 106, 114
coihue de Magallanes 8, 36 (*map*), 37, 40

coihue-raulí-tepa forest 5, 8, 10 (map), 20 (*map*), 22, 24, 34, 35
colihue 42
colocolo 93
colonial Chile 65
commercially productive forest 62, 66, 69
commercially valuable native trees 61
CONAF (Corporación Nacional Forestal) x, 2, 4, 6, 31, 46, 53, 55, 58, 60, 61, 66-69, 74, 76, 77, 80, 81, 89, 94, 96, 100, 105, 108, 109, 114, 120, 121, 123, 124, 133
Concepción 47
conifers 14
conquistadors 1, 39, 67
conservation of biodiversity 83-94, 105, 107
Conservation International 118, 127
Contao River 114
Contramaestre Island 112
Convention on International Trade in Endangered Species (CITES) 28, 67
Convention for the Protection of Flora, Fauna and Scenic Beauty 67
Convention on Biological Diversity 118
conversion of native forests to plantations 48, 49, 58, 67, 113, 114, 117
copihue 26, 34, 84
cordilleran cypress 14, 30, 33, 34, 61, 89, 90
cordilleran cypress forest 8, 10 (*map*), 14
Cordoba Ravine 112
CORMA 119
corporate ownership of forests 56
Coscoroba swan 95
Cruces River 111
Cudico 111
cypress 33
cyttaria fungus 35
Darwin, Charles 44, 71
Darwin's frog 35, 110
Decree Law 701 47, 65
Defensores del Bosque Chileno vii, xi, 132
deforestation 2-5, 12, 46, 48, 65, 84, 86, 97, 116, 118, 130, 131
degraded forests 3, 11, 14, 15, 44, 48, 51, 66, 69, 73, 103, 105, 109, 113
Diego Ramirez Islands 111
distribution of protected areas 76, 109
domestic livestock 35
Donoso, Claudio 4, 45, 109
Douglas fir 29, 30, 47
dwarf canelo 26, 40, 42
early land use regulations 65
earthquakes 96
Easter Island 86
Ecoforestry Institute 118, 120
ecological subregions 86
ecological sustainability 104, 118
economic development 49, 115, 118
ecosystem diversity 85
ecosystem-based management 5, 58, 60, 113
ecotourism 104, 120, 121-127